power surge

six marks of Discipleship for a changing church

Michael W. Foss

FORTRESS PRESS   MINNEAPOLIS

For Christine

My lifelong partner and wife,
who has encouraged me to follow my passion
for mission-based ministry
for more than thirty years.
Her wisdom, counsel,
and spiritual discernment have,
to a large degree, made this book possible.

Cover design by David Meyer
Book design by Michelle L. Norstad

Library of Congress Cataloging-in-Publication Data
Foss, Michael W., 1948–
    Power surge : six marks of discipleship for a changing church / Michael W. Foss.
        p. cm.
    Includes bibliographical references.
    ISBN 0-8006-3264-8 (alk. paper)
    1. Church renewal. I. Title.

BV600.2.F67 2000
269–dc21   00-037119

The paper used in this publication meets the minimum requirements of American National Standard for Information Sciences–Permanence of Paper for Printed Library Materials, ANSI Z329.48-1984. ⊖ ™

Manufactured in the U.S.A.   AF 1-3264
09   08   07   13   14   15   16   17   18

Contents

Acknowledgments

The writing of any book is a collaborative project. I begin by acknowledging the significant work of my editor and friend, Dr. Henry French of Augsburg Fortress Publishers. His dedication and encouragement have been very important to me in the process of writing and publication.

I also want to thank the staff, members, and friends of Prince of Peace Lutheran Church in Burnsville, Minnesota. Without their participation in the congregation's significant shift from membership to discipleship, the ideas within this book would not have been tested and developed to the point of being worth sharing with you. These ideas have emerged from the crucible of ministry; I cannot claim them as my own. They belong to the Holy Spirit, working through all of us at Prince of Peace as we have continued to grow together.

I also want to thank my two daughters, Sarah and Linnea, who have so wonderfully and freely shared with me the perspectives of another generation of believers who struggle to find a home for their convictions.

introduction

"I don't know how to minister anymore," the senior pastor of a flagging mainline church lamented. "There was a time when faithfully preaching and teaching God's word was enough. But no matter how much time I spend preparing and working to communicate the gospel, it just doesn't seem to make any difference. And I know that I'm not alone, either. Most of my colleagues are just biding their time until they can retire."

He looked down for a moment and then wearily continued, "It's not that we don't believe anymore, not even that we don't care. It's that we simply don't know what to do and we're tired—I'm tired—of beating my head against a brick wall."

There is no denying it: ministry in the Protestant church at the beginning of the twenty-first century is difficult. A spirit of frustration and despair afflicts many of the church's finest leaders. What once worked no longer appears effective, and many who are charged with the leadership of God's people are at a loss as to what to do. Like a ship without a rudder, the church flounders in dangerous waters.

There is a vacuum of vision, of ideas and strategies with which to respond to the growing disparity between the life and ministry of the congregation and the real lives of people in our society. The connection between the faith of the church and the life of the people is strained to the breaking point, and harried pastors and lay leaders burn out at an alarming rate as they struggle to keep the church from losing all relevance in our postmodern world.

Christian leaders are looking for new, dynamic, and effective ways of being the church, ways that are faithful to the call of God and that will energize them and their ministries. Pastors and lay leaders are longing for a spiritual spark to ignite the passions of God's people once again. This deep longing on the part of Christian leaders is accompanied by a growing sense of urgency, a growing sense that the time may be running out on American Protestantism.

Pastor and sociologist Bill Easum, noted lecturer and student of the Protestant church internationally, has said, "Most mainline and established churches are dying because *they only try to take care of their members.* Three out of four will close over the next 25–30 years. . . . Most mainline churches are already irrelevant to the needs of postmodern people."[1]

Others have suggested that one-third of the more than 325,000 Protestant congregations in the United States will close their doors within the next decade. And that is a conservative estimate!

Consider the following sobering statistics:

- 91 percent of all households in the United States own at least one Bible
- 80 percent of adults name the Bible as the most influential book in human history
- Yet only 38 percent of adults read the Bible in any given week
- Only 25 percent of adults volunteer to help a church during a typical week
- 96 percent of adults believe in God
- 93 percent believe in the virgin birth
- Yet 39 percent say Jesus did not have a physical resurrection
- 61 percent say that the Holy Spirit is not real
- 56 percent say a good person can earn his or her way into heaven
- And still 72 percent of those polled say that they are church members[2]

What is going on here? How has it happened? And what can we do about it? Why is biblical illiteracy rampant among those who call themselves Christian? Why does the Christian message, the good news of the gospel, not seem to get through? Why are all the mainline Protestant churches losing more and more of their members? Is Christian faith no longer relevant? Is the church no longer effective in meeting the real needs of real people? These are questions that trouble the hearts and minds of all who love and serve the Lord of the church. They are questions I shall address in this book.

MODELS OF CHURCH AFFILIATION

The world has changed faster than the church, and now it is time for the church to catch up and learn to speak and act in ways that the world can understand. The Christian message remains as true and relevant today as it has ever been. The gospel of Jesus Christ still answers to the deep hopes and fears, the realities and dreams of men, women, and children in each and every walk of life. In a pick-and-choose, mix-and-match spiritual marketplace, staggering in its diversity and complexity, Christian faith, Christian spirituality is not reducible to just one among many religious commodities. Christian faith is not an accessory to life. Rather it is a coherent way of life, a way of being in the world. It is the task of the church to teach and support this way of life, this life of the spirit, for the sake of individuals and communities.

The methods and strategies that effectively served to teach and support the life of faith in the past now seem outworn and unable to address the critical issues of our time. The church seems increasingly powerless, and we who serve the church in this challenging time wrestle like Jacob with the angel, seeking a blessing, trying desperately to be and remain relevant, wondering where the needed power surge will come from.

Let me suggest that all the power the church will ever need comes from people—people who have learned to live "in Christ" by living lives of disciplined discipleship. The resurrected Jesus told his earliest followers to "go therefore and make disciples [not church members] of all nations . . . teaching them to obey everything that I have commanded you" (Matthew 28:19-20). And what had he commanded them? What were they to teach these new disciples? In a word, love. "I give you a new commandment, that you love one another. Just as I have loved you, you also should love one another. By this *everyone will know that you are my disciples, if you have love for one another*" (John 13:34-35, emphasis added).

All the power the church will ever need, all the relevance the church will ever need, comes from people who love because they live consciously as disciples of the risen Christ. When we teach, train, equip, empower, encourage, support, and challenge people in their calling as disciples of the risen Christ, the power of Christ's life surges through the church and wonderful, grace-full, life-giving, life-celebrating things begin to happen.

We are long overdue for a paradigm shift in American Protestantism—a shift from a membership model of church affiliation to a discipleship model. As important as the notion of church membership may have been in years past, it no longer works. Churches are losing members in droves. All too many folks whose names still fill churches' membership rolls have long since slipped out the back door. The two most common reasons given: burnout and boredom.

All too many churches are experiencing an unprecedented erosion of loyalty to the congregation itself. Active members not only give less time than ever before to the life and ministries of the church, but they consider themselves active when they worship only once or twice a month. Recent studies indicate that as many as one out of three active families in the average congregation is seriously considering changing its church affiliation. That this is accurate is demonstrated by the great numbers of active members who use a local change of residence to exit their church. Although they continue to live within easy driving distance of their former congregation, their move gives them permission to leave without guilt. And leave they do. There are also great numbers of individuals and families who consider themselves members of a congregation but who rarely or never attend worship beyond weddings and funerals, Christmas, and Easter.

Church membership has lost much of its claim on the lives of today's Christians.

As the notion of church membership has become increasingly meaningless in American society, church membership has lost much of its claim on the lives of today's Christians.

Organizational affiliations are casual for many individuals, and a significant number of Christians view the church as just one more of these affiliations. This seems to be the only possible explanation for the high percentage of North American adults who nominally claim to be Christian but whose beliefs have little or no power to shape their lives, let alone add value or significance to their families and communities.

ANOTHER SIDE TO THE STORY

But there is another side to this story. When congregations stop focusing on membership and reclaim the dynamics of discipleship, things begin to change.

A rural congregation made the courageous decision to commit their meager resources to mission instead of maintenance. When they sold their property and stately church, the only building they could find for worship was a store in town that fronted Main Street. The first Sunday they opened for worship in this "secular" setting, the congregation had visitors for the first time in—well, they couldn't remember. And they had not one or two visitors but sixty-three new worshipers that Sunday.

It was a painful, difficult process that led them to the momentous decision to sell their old country church and move downtown into mission. After all, that old, beautiful, but hard-to-maintain church building was where many of them had been baptized, where their children had been confirmed and married, where their parent's funerals had been held. But the congregation had a new vision for discipleship. And they decided to follow that costly vision.

"I can't believe how much fun I'm having!" exclaimed a young pastor who had taken up ministry in a metropolitan area only three years before. "We're adding another service, and I'm adding a new worship director to our staff. People are coming to worship—even when I tell them the hard truth! I haven't watered down anything. I just ask those that come to seriously reflect on what I say and then pray and make up their own minds. If they see the truth of it, *then they should live it*. So far, God has blessed us incredibly. And we're changing lives, making disciples by the power of the gospel." The congregation had made the decision to stop turning in and start turning out—a move from maintenance to mission, from membership to discipleship.

A mainline pastor remarked, "When we became a 'high expectation' congregation, the first to experience its joy were the leaders. We began to hold ourselves, our relationships and vocations, accountable to our spirituality. The next to discover the power of discipleship were our new members. They had chosen to affiliate with us because they want their faith to shape their lives. The energy this has given our church is incredible. Ministry matters. The Bible is the Book of Life, not just something to have in your home. And I no longer carry the church on my own shoulders." This pastor was celebrating a spiritual renewal within his congregation, a renewal characterized by continually increasing worship attendance as more and more people responded to the magnetic attraction of committed discipleship.

The goal is discipleship. The critical issue is leadership. How shall leaders in Christ's church grow disciples of Christ in the next decades? What can or ought leaders expect of those who claim membership in their congregations or ministries? How can the ministry of Christ's church equip God's people to participate in God's love for the world in all the places where they live and work and play? What spiritual disciplines can support the leaders of the church so that all people will know they are Christ's disciples—not by their titles, but by their love? What are the marks of discipleship that characterize both those who lead the church and those who follow them?

In this book, I speak to leaders of both large and small congregations, drawing on my experience as senior pastor of Prince of Peace Lutheran Church in Burnsville, Minnesota. As it is at Prince of Peace, so I believe it is everywhere: Christians are being called to a new (or perhaps I should say renewed) vision of what it means to be a part of the body of Christ, the church in the world. The collapse of the membership model of church affiliation demands a new model of leadership. Ordained pastors, nonordained professionals in ministry, and volunteer lay leaders must, above all, be disciples themselves. The minister as manager, the pastor as CEO, the leader as "the authority" are models of church leadership that are not worthy of the one who emptied himself and took the form of a servant (Philippians 2:7). The leader as disciple—as one who loves—and as a mentor of disciples—a mentor of those who love—is exactly what Jesus of Nazareth had in mind for his followers.

> Christians are being called to a new vision of what it means to be a part of the body of Christ, the church in the world.

To move from a membership to a discipleship model of the church can cause extraordinary stress to organizations, systems, and those that lead them. But it is an experience of extraordinary opportunity, as well. In the confidence of the Holy Spirit, I believe Christian leaders can be spiritually renewed and equipped for mentoring congregations into a new age of effective ministry and faithful discipleship.

But first, the old must give way to the new in the heart and mind of the leader. That is the exercise to which you are invited in the following pages. And along the way, I will introduce you to the six marks of discipleship that have brought a power surge to Prince of Peace and that hold the same promise for any church that makes the move from membership to discipleship.

1
making the move
from membership
to discipleship

It was one of those moments I'll never forget. It happened on a Sunday in spring, and like the season, it too had to do with newness.

My associate pastor and I found we worked well together as a team, and our congregation's membership was nearing one thousand people. We felt both grateful and confident. On this particular Sunday, however, I was in for a shock. As I looked out with pride on that growing, vibrant, worshipful congregation, I suddenly realized that there were individuals and families who were joining the church whose names I did not know, in whose homes I had not visited. I was stunned. I felt as if the world had changed overnight and I was just discovering it. I was shaken to the core, because my guiding model of ministry—that of being a personal pastor for each parishioner—was no longer viable.

My model for ministry also included focusing on church growth through increasing membership. Evangelism was a matter of bringing people into the church and then tending to their spiritual needs. But how could I do that if I didn't even know them? My associate was very capable. He'd been in many of their homes and knew many of their names. But, as he later confessed, many he didn't know well at all.

Although I didn't realize it at the time, my paradigm for ministry was being significantly challenged. That Sunday, with its sudden insight, was the beginning of my move from a focus on membership to a focus on discipleship.

My training had taught me only one way to do ministry and to judge its effectiveness—call it the *membership model* of ministry. If the membership was growing and happy—and they seemed to be—then my ministry was successful. The model with which I had been working wasn't all about numbers, though. I also assumed that the pastoral staff's effective pastoral care was a necessary element to our spiritual health and vitality. I assumed that personally knowing the names and families and, as much as possible, the histories of those who attended and joined our church was an essential element in my ministry. I taught confirmation, attended the women's lunches, played golf and racquetball with the men, led a number of Bible studies—all in an attempt to be a *personal pastor* to as many as possible.

In a growing church with more and more members to be served, this is a certain prescription for clergy burnout. The reason many churches don't grow—or stop growing—is that the pastoral staff reaches its limit for personal care and then, consciously or unconsciously, creates a climate and systems that discourage growth.

Roots of the Membership Model

For decades, the membership model of the church has dominated American Protestantism. That model lingers as an adaptation of the village church system that existed in premodern western Europe. In the village, the pastor or priest served as the holy man for the whole community. He was responsible for serving the spiritual and often material needs of parish families at important life passages, such as birth, confirmation, marriage, critical illness or injury, and death.

The relationships of individuals and families to God were mediated through the rites of the church as administered by the village pastor. The pastor received a certain amount of prestige and the power that goes with it—often a great deal, depending upon his abilities—and the people received the assurance of connectedness to God as the pastor shared the sacraments, led worship, provided personal pastoral care, and in general tended to the spiritual life of the community.

To be a pastor or priest also was to be in the center of village life. A pastor's relationship to the village served as a cohesive force in the identity of the community, and the pastor often played an important role in affirming and upholding the identity of individuals and families as members of the church and citizens of the village itself. Beliefs, values, and behaviors were articulated by the clergy in ways that shaped the larger community as well as the church. As such, the ministry of the church and the role of the clergy functioned like social glue as well as a source of spiritual solace.

For many modern Christians, particularly in the post–World War II era, the membership model of the church functioned in an analogous way. The congregation provided social as well as spiritual connections. Church was a place to meet others with whom one could confidently do business, share friendship, and uphold similar values. There were clear understandings of what membership in such a community of faith required. It meant giving some of one's time and finances to keep the organization going and to pay the pastor's salary. It meant not only accepting that ministry belonged to the minister but also expecting to be ministered to. It meant acting in a manner consistent with conventional morality and appropriate behavior. Church membership was akin to good citizenship. It created a significant sense of personal identity, and with that came the confidence that the church was both preserving values that were necessary for the health of the larger community and nation as well as playing an important role in efforts to improve society.

No wonder the post–World War II years saw an explosion in the number of congregations in the United States. The successful completion of the war itself was understood to have been accomplished through a sturdy faith in God and the concerted effort of Americans working together for a common goal. The individual, it was understood, could make his or her best contribution by being a contributing member of a group, and the membership of the mainline churches grew exponentially.

The social and spiritual messages of the Protestant churches, their professionalized ministries, and their organizational structures were well suited for that time—and for years to come. I and many of my colleagues were effective doing ministry in this mode. Until recently, the churches grew and, we believed, our communities, nation, and world benefited from that growth.

But times have changed. The church and its clergy have lost their privileged positions at the center of community life; hundreds of civic and social organizations compete for the time, talents, and finances of the citizenry; postmodern pluralism has relativized every belief and value system so that the faith is reduced to a commodity in the religious marketplace.

For all too many today, Christianity is at best parochial and quaint (read irrelevant) and at worst dangerously intolerant. And for most in our culture, religion of whatever brand has been reduced to the private sphere of life. The gospel as public faith, sadly, seems a contradiction in terms.

In the Protestant explosion of the 1950s, membership implied obligation. In today's cultural context, membership has come to imply prerogatives.

The changing cultural context, with its displacement of Christianity from the center of individual and community life to the periphery, has caused a mutation in the membership model of the church. In the Protestant explosion of the 1950s, membership implied obligation. In today's cultural context, membership has come to imply prerogatives.

I don't want to push the analogy too far, but for the sake of illustration, let's think of the membership model of the church as similar to the membership model of a modern health club. One becomes a member of a health club by paying dues (in a church, the monthly or weekly offering). Having paid their dues, the members expect the services of the club to be at their disposal. Exercise equipment, weight room, aerobics classes, an indoor track, swimming pool—all there for them, with a trained staff to see that they benefit by them. Members may bring a guest on occasion, but only those who pay their dues have a right to the use of the facilities and the attention of the staff. There is no need to belabor the point. Many of the people who sit in the pews on Sunday have come to think of church membership in ways analogous to how the fitness crowd views membership in a health club.

The tragic flaw in the contemporary version of the membership model of the church lies in the focus of its ministry. In that model, ministry focuses on the *membership* of a particular congregation. With the member as the focal point, the role of the clergy is to meet the spiritual needs of the members, keep the members happy, and generally do ministry in ways that make as few waves as possible. If the members' perceived needs are adequately met, if they are happy with the services provided by the professional staff, and if conflict is avoided or minimized, then the membership can be counted on to do their part. Their part, of course, is to pay their "dues," to keep the offering flowing that pays the bills, salaries, and costs of ministry.

You can see why the membership model of ministry is also called the maintenance model of ministry. Maintaining the institution for the sake of its members is the primary goal—whether stated or not—of the congregation.

I don't want to be harsh. Under the membership model of the church, hardworking, faithful clergy have met the spiritual needs of their members in often heroic and heartwarming ways. The church has been there for its people at those signal times of life when connectedness to God is most needed. The church has been a comfortable and comforting place for many people, although their numbers are clearly diminishing. The membership model has had its strengths as well as its weaknesses.

> Perhaps the greatest weakness of the membership model has been the loss, over time, of its vision for the mission of the church.

Perhaps the greatest weakness of the model has been the loss, over time, of its vision for the mission of the church—a mission that can be characterized quite simply as participation in God's love in Jesus Christ for the world. As the membership model gradually changed its focal point from the mission of the church to the member of the church, the church was tamed, privatized, turned in on itself. Powerful individuals and families—including clergy!—were able to control the ministry of a congregation according to their private agendas. Instead of a people organized for mission, the churches frequently became institutions organized for those already there. Decisions could be made with little or no reference to the church's role in the world as the historical presence of Christ.

As a product of the membership model for ministry—by nurture as well as by training—I read the Great Commission as if it had been written, "Go therefore and make *members* of all nations, baptizing them in the name of the Father and the Son and the Holy Spirit, teaching them to observe all that I have commanded you." But, of course, that is not how it reads. The critical word is *disciples*. Disciples are those who are both baptized and taught to observe what Jesus has commanded his followers. And that, as noted in the introduction, means to love in his name and spirit. Being a part of the church has little or nothing to do with prerogatives or privileged status except in one regard—disciples *know* that they are infinitely loved by the God who made them. They know that being a part of the church, the community of faith, has to do with being loved and loving, that is, with discipleship.

THE MEMBERSHIP MODEL
IN MICROCOSM

"We just have too few of us to do the job anymore," the chair of the altar guild had come to me to say. "And, Pastor, we're tired."

I knew that their numbers were few and older. I also knew that those numbers could be increased and given a youthful energy with careful recruitment of some of our newer members who were eager to become involved.

"I'll tell you what," I responded. "Let me see if a couple of women who have recently joined the church might be interested. I'll let you know."

"Pastor," she said, "that would be great."

But it wasn't. Two months later three women, all new members, joined the altar guild. Three months after that, they had all resigned. When I asked each of them why they had left the guild, they all said the same thing: "The other women didn't really want us to help."

I knew it wasn't intentional. The members of our altar guild were fine people, but they had their own ways of doing things, their own comfort with working with one another. Later, I realized that they were a microcosm of the congregation. They had formed their own fellowship group—a group that didn't need, or want, any new members. They shared a friendship and history with one another that centered in the "work" of the guild. It is no wonder the newcomers felt left out.

What is important to recognize in this story is how the mission of the guild had become secondary to the comfort of the group's members. The truth was that they were indeed overworked! But in my attempts to solve their problem, I had miscalculated the power of their "membership" to dictate how, when, and by whom their work was done. I believe that if I could have redirected their attention to the mission they shared and convinced them that, for the sake of their mission to the larger church community, they needed to become involved in recruiting, welcoming, and mentoring others, then the "hazing" described by those other women would have been less likely to happen.

Let me hasten to add that this is but one illustration of the power of the membership model. It happens in every congregation where the membership and its prerogatives are the lens through which issues are seen and solutions presented.

No wonder the few who seem to be "always doing the work" are most visible in our ministries—they are in the center of our membership!

At Prince of Peace, we recently studied the involvement of individuals in our various ministries. We discovered that, conservatively, we were benefiting from 5,400 hours of volunteer effort every week. We estimated that these hours of lay ministry are given by more than 4,000 different individuals. Our move from membership to discipleship, though by no means complete, has led to a congregation of vibrant, involved, growing disciples of Christ.

EXCLUSIVITY VERSUS INCLUSIVITY

Another problem with the membership model is its tendency to define the congregation *exclusively* rather than *inclusively*. The membership model identifies who is in and who is out. No wonder then that those outside the church consistently say that church people are more judgmental than others. No wonder that those for whom the front door of the church is a revolving door often say that the reason they don't stay is the lack of genuine hospitality. They don't feel genuinely welcomed, wanted, or needed.

That is not to say that church people are cold, indifferent, or unfriendly. My experience is just the opposite. Rather, it is the system that is not friendly. The membership model sets the church over against those outside the membership. The whole notion of the "church for others" gets lost, and people act, both consciously and unconsciously, to protect the "church for ourselves."

The sense of exclusivity that the church portrays under the membership model is a key factor in discouraging postmodern seekers from crossing the threshold, coming inside, and staying around long enough to hear and experience the gospel of God's love. The postmodern impulse in the United States is creating a people that highly values tolerance, uncritical acceptance of others, and a great plurality of beliefs, values, and behaviors. In this social reality, it therefore should come as no shock that membership in our churches continues to decline. The perception that the church doesn't embrace outsiders undermines our credibility. What we need to communicate to those outside the church is radical openness to all, an openness extended from a position of strong, vibrant self-identity as followers of Christ and participants in God's love for the world. That's what the discipleship model of the church gives us.

The United States has become a pluralistic country that no longer consciously subscribes to the Judeo-Christian ethic summed up in the Great Commandment: "You shall love the Lord your God with all your heart, and with all your soul, and with all your mind. This is the greatest and first commandment. And a second is like it: You shall love your neighbor as yourself" (Matthew 22:36-40). Hence the incredible need for disciples of Christ in all walks of life who have internalized and live that ethic and whose lives witness to the wonder and truth of it.

Discipleship is about changing and shaping lives by the grace of God.

The Protestant church has focused on itself—for that is what the membership model requires—and our core beliefs are not served by that orientation. Our core beliefs turn us outwards, not inwards. The membership model of the church turns us inwards and not outwards, and as Martin Luther once noted, sin is the state of being curved in on yourself!

Over the years, I have time and again invited folks who have been worshiping with us and contributing in many ways to the life of the congregation to join, only to be asked, "What do I get as a member that I don't get now?"

Membership is about getting; discipleship is about giving. Membership is about dues; discipleship is about stewardship. Membership is about belonging to a select group with its privileges and prerogatives; discipleship is about changing and shaping lives by the grace of God.

THE MOVE TO DISCIPLESHIP

The move from membership to discipleship is not easy. Trying to change the mind-set, values, and behavior patterns of any community is difficult at best and perilous at worst. But it can be done, over time and incrementally. It has happened before.

When the early church was trying to sort itself out with respect to who was in and who was out, the prevailing attitude was that Jews were in and Gentiles were out. The early church was a fairly closed community, worshiping in Jewish synagogues and private homes, following Jewish laws and rites. According to the book of Acts, one day Peter, who had been praying, fell into a trance. "He saw the heaven opened and something like a large sheet coming down, being lowered to the ground by its four corners. In it were all kinds of four-footed creatures and reptiles and birds of the air." Peter heard a voice telling him to "kill and eat." He refused, arguing that it was against Jewish law to eat "unclean" animals. The voice from heaven commanded again, saying: "What God has made clean, you must not call profane."

The vision ended, and Peter was summoned to the home of Cornelius, a Gentile who was drawn to the worship of God and who wanted to learn more about the faith of the early church. Peter did the previously unthinkable. Following the Spirit of Christ, he entered the Gentile's house. Apparently he had got the point of his vision. He said to Cornelius and his household, "You yourself know that it is unlawful for a Jew to associate with or to visit a Gentile; but God has shown me that I should not call anyone profane or unclean" (Acts 10:1-48).

The impact of Peter's move from exclusivity to inclusivity, from defending the prerogatives of membership to extending the grace of God, from narrow sectarianism to an open embrace of the world God loves turned the fledgling church upside down and inside out. To be sure, it wasn't easy. The book of Acts records the conflicts and continuing debates and disputes over the move from membership to discipleship, and any church today that seeks to make a similar move can expect much of the same.

Old ways of thinking, believing, and behaving do not change easily, but they do change when, like Peter, God's people follow the Spirit of Christ and attempt the previously unthinkable. Doing so takes courage, but we need to remind ourselves that we have the courage needed: "for God did not give us a spirit of cowardice, but rather a spirit of power and of love and of self-discipline" (2 Timothy 1:7).

An ancient Chinese proverb reminds us that "the journey of a thousand miles begins with a single step." The journey from membership to discipleship is arduous and long, but its ending is in its beginning—the choice to make the move!

QUESTIONS FOR PRAYERFUL REFLECTION

1. Would you describe your congregation as internally or externally focused? How do you know?

2. Does the pastoral and other salaried staff in your congregation spend most of their time doing ministry or mentoring others in ministry?

3. Given the size of your congregation, has the pastoral and other salaried staff reached the limits of ministry in terms of their time, energy, and ability? Are things not getting done? Is growth stymied? Is anyone in danger of burnout?

4. Does the membership model of the church and ministry greatly describe, somewhat describe, or not describe your congregation?

5. Does beginning the move from membership to discipleship make sense for your congregation? Why or why not?

6. If your congregation were to decide to undertake a move to a discipleship model, what barriers to change can you envision?

7. In the life of faith, all things begin and end in prayer. Take a moment now to speak with God about what's going through your mind, your heart, your spirit as you reflect on the present realities of your congregation.

THE JOURNEY OF A THOUSAND
MILES BEGINS WITH A SINGLE STEP.

2 Discipleship and spiritual leadership

I had been at St. Matthew Lutheran Church for just a few months when I received the late-night phone call. I was informed that one of our church council members (let's call her Shirley) was going in for major surgery in the morning. I thanked the caller (why, I wondered to myself, hadn't Shirley let me know of her need?) and then set my alarm clock. To a night owl, the prospect of getting up by 5:15 A.M. in order to make it to the hospital early enough to read Scripture and pray with this member was not exciting—but it was necessary.

In the morning, I donned my clerical attire and headed down the hill to the hospital, which I had visited only a few times before. I parked in the ramp and, as I entered the lobby of the hospital, made the first of a number of discoveries: there is no one at the reception desk at 5:30 in the morning. As I wandered about, a nurse came to my rescue and, accessing the hospital's computer records, told me where and how to find Shirley.

I walked down the darkened hospital corridor, checked in at the nurses' station, and received directions to Shirley's room. As I turned the corner of the hallway to her room, I looked up and saw another member of the church walking down the hallway. Just as I noticed her, she noticed me.

"Why, Pastor Mike, what are you doing here?" she asked.

I answered that I had come to see Shirley, to which she replied, "Oh, of course. We just didn't expect to see you." And then she led me to Shirley's room.

As I entered, I saw Wendy, another member of our church, sitting on the bed with Shirley, holding her hand and speaking softly with her. When Wendy looked up and saw me, she too asked, "Pastor Mike, what are *you* doing here?" By now this was becoming a bit tedious.

"Well," I said as pleasantly as I could muster at that hour of the morning, "I am here to see Shirley before surgery."

At that point, Wendy got up from the hospital bed, stepped back and, as I stepped forward, Shirley greeted me and told me how glad she was that I had come.

As I extended my hand to Shirley, the other two women began to leave the room, saying, "Well, we'll leave you alone with Shirley."

But I asked them to stay while I read Scripture. We then joined hands, and I led a prayer for Shirley and her surgery. I was doing my job, providing pastoral care, being the presence of the church for Shirley in her moment of need.

But driving away from the hospital, I had a nagging thought: "Did you see what you just did?" that inner voice asked.

"Yes," I smugly replied to the voice. "I just did a fine piece of pastoral care early in the morning."

"But did you see what you did?" the question returned. And in my mind's eye, I saw the displacement of two women from their friend's side. I saw how I had, unintentionally, moved them away in order for me to do my ministry. In the membership model of the church, the pastor functions like a private chaplain for the church's members. That, without thinking, is what I had been up to with Shirley.

And then that inner voice returned. "Do you really believe that I listen to your prayers more than theirs?"

Changes of perspective rarely come because they are a good idea. They arise out of unavoidable shocks to the status quo. From some of these shocks we recover fairly quickly and the world easily comes back into focus. From others, such as this personal experience, we often are left confused and questioning for a long time.

My own response was first to pray and confess my own arrogance in ministry and then, secondly, to ponder what it might mean for the future of my ministry. My conclusion was that I was being divinely invited to a new way of doing ministry, one that valued the faith, gifts, and ministry of all of God's people. How that would happen and what it would mean for the congregation was beyond my imagination at that time. But another step on the journey from membership to discipleship had been taken.

AN OLD TREASURE FOR A NEW TIME

"And Jesus said to them, "Therefore every scribe who has been trained for the kingdom of heaven is like the master of a household who brings out of his treasure what is new and what is old" (Matthew 13:52).

Discipleship is an old treasure that those of us who have been trained for the kingdom of heaven need to pull out, dust off, and commend to the "members" of our congregations. It is an old treasure that can be dressed in the new clothes of contemporary strategies, methods, and technologies.

Discipleship is about individual Christians—and the church as a community of Christians—living in mission.

Discipleship is about following in the way of Jesus Christ. It is no accident that the earliest disciples were called "people of the Way" long before they were first called "Christians." Discipleship is about individual Christians—and the church as a community of Christians—living in mission. Discipleship is about recognizing that Christ is in the center of both personal and public life and then living out the implications of that reality.

I am not suggesting that, under the membership model of the church, Christian leaders intentionally moved Christ from the center to the periphery of congregational, private, or public life. I am suggesting, however, that a church structure whose primary focus is on the member rather than on the mission quite naturally and inevitably de-centers both Christ and the mission of God to the world. Such a model for ministry subtly but surely moves the ownership of the church from the Lord of the church to the member of the church.

This was not the primary model of the early church. For the first three centuries of the Christian church's existence, membership was the consequence of discipleship. Only with the adoption of Christianity by the Roman Emperor Constantine in the fourth century, and the consequent "socializing" of the faith, did membership in the church become a possibility for those who had not already been moved by the Holy Spirit to become disciples of Christ.

Though discipleship continued to be called for by the great leaders of the church throughout the centuries after Constantine, it was no longer expected of ordinary Christians. Discipleship certainly wasn't necessary to become a Christian, that is, a member of the church. National identity, cultural assimilation, and profession of belief in a set of dogmas displaced discipleship as the prerequisites for membership.

No wonder the desert fathers and mothers fled into the wilderness to nurture their longing for discipleship—a daily way of living that acknowledges Christ as the center of life. Though we might disagree with some of their theology and practice, we cannot help but admire their single-minded focus in pursuing the life of faith as followers of Christ.[3]

No wonder, on the other hand, that within a few hundred years, the chaplaincy model of ministry, which grows necessarily out of the membership model of the church, had so taken root that Pope Gregory the Great (ca. 540–604) standardized its practice in his book *Pastoral Rule*. With that work, the membership model became entrenched in the Western church, and, as they say, the rest is history.

But it need not be the history of our congregations. We can, as Christ teaches, go back to get to our future and reclaim for today the old treasure of discipleship as the primary reason for being a part of the church, that is, the body of Christ.

DISTINGUISHING FORM FROM FAITH

On a plane, Wayne Hammit found himself seated next to a man from the Middle East. In the course of conversation, that man learned Wayne's name and immediately identified that it, too, was Middle Eastern. Wayne explained that he had become a Christian and was now a Lutheran pastor. At that point the man sitting next to him shared that he was an

Arab Jew. He went on to explain that both he and his father had carefully read both the Old and the New Testaments. They believed, this gentleman declared softly, that there was no doubt that Jesus was the messiah.

On hearing that, Wayne exclaimed, "Then you must be a Christian, too!"

The man exploded, vehemently and loudly denying this assertion.

Wayne waited for him to quiet down and then asked a series of questions to discover why this man who believed Jesus of Nazareth was the messiah would so loudly deny the faith that asserted that very thing. In the end, he learned it was because the man couldn't separate Christianity from American culture. It wasn't the faith he felt he had to deny but the form he understood was necessary for that faith.

The discipleship model seeks to distinguish form from faith, container from content. It insists that form follows function, not that form determines and limits function. In the story of Peter and Cornelius in the book of Acts, the form of the early church, with its exclusive membership, would have prevented Peter from responding to the spiritual needs of Cornelius, an "outsider." The form of the church would have encouraged Peter to see Cornelius as an object against which to discriminate rather than as a subject of God's love.

When form follows function (which is another way of saying when the church follows the Spirit, as Peter did), form takes the shape that love and justice require. Perhaps if discipleship, rather than membership, determined the form of the church, Wayne Hammit's airplane companion would not have needed to respond the way he did.

Pastors Are Leaders, Not Chaplains

The pastoral role in the discipleship model is a function of leadership, not chaplaincy. This doesn't mean that the pastoral needs of the congregation and its constituents are not of great concern for the pastor, staff, and lay leaders. But those needs are addressed within and by the community of faith itself. Additionally, there is a clear understanding that meeting the needs of those within the church is best accomplished when the local church is in mission and attempting to meet the needs of those outside the church.

The mission of God is the context for meeting the needs of those who worship within and affiliate with the church. This meeting of needs only becomes possible when Christ is acknowledged as being at the center of everything—be it inside or outside the church. The how of the ministry is a matter of leadership that can only be effectively addressed within the context of ministry carried out in obedience to Christ's mission.

The problem is, of course, that the functions of leadership are not well understood. Leaders, according to John Kotter of the Harvard Business School, function quite differently from managers. Leaders are responsible to provide vision, raise up other leaders, and *create useful change*. Managers, however, *maintain* the present system and seek to enhance it. Sadly, most church leaders are, in reality, managers.[4]

Leaders understand that the vitality of any organization, including the Christian church, is directly related to the level of expectation the organization sets before its constituents. Discipleship as a model for ministry raises the bar—not to the level of perfection, but to the level of *passionate followership*. In most of the Protestant churches in North America, this would be a radical change of expectation.

Passionate followers of Jesus Christ cannot and do not separate their lives into the timeworn categories of the sacred and the secular. All is sacred, for Christ is present wherever they are. Faith and life constantly intersect. Indeed, faith and life are indistinguishable for the passionate follower, the disciple of Christ, and it is the calling of Christian leaders to equip their people for this life of faith—a life lived mostly outside the four walls of the church.

In the membership model of the church, with its chaplaincy model of ministry, the pastor functions as a family or individual caregiver. The pastor is expected to meet individual parishioners in their time of need and bring to their person or their family the spiritual resources of the church. The pastor is the prayer, the reader of Scripture, the point at which heaven touches earth.

In the discipleship model, the pastor still may do these things, but with the intent of modeling the constant intersecting of life with the Spirit and so mentoring people in the life of the Spirit. The aim is to practice the art of spiritual care in such a way as to connect individuals with their own spiritual resources and the strength and power of their own prayers. Instead of being intermediaries, pastors become spiritual catalysts through whom the Holy Spirit encourages, equips, directs, and strengthens the faith of those they serve. There is a significant shift of intent here. The pastor strives to get out of the way of ministry, not in a passive manner, but in an active and intentional way. The goal is shared ministry: all of God's people living their faith, using their gifts, making Christ present to one another through compassion, love, and service. The center of ministry is Christ

> **Pastors become spiritual catalysts through whom the Holy Spirit encourages, equips, directs, and strengthens the faith of those they serve.**

and the Savior's presence within each of us, to each of us, through each of us at all times.

One of the great tragedies of the chaplaincy model is that it sets pastors up for failure. No matter how committed pastors may be, there is simply no way they can always be present in times of need. Times of crisis come when the family or individual least expects them. Pastors are often not immediately available or may be so exhausted or so pressed for time that, even when they are available, they are not entirely there. But Christ is—always available, always powerful.

The power of our faith is not inaccessible whenever and wherever the professional religious person is inaccessible. Quite to the contrary. Whenever and wherever any followers of Christ are present to another in intentionally loving and caring ways, Christ is present and faith is both active and powerful.

When the pastor is the primary doer of ministry, the community's presence is reduced to one or two or three. Though unintended, the absence of the pastor in times of crisis or need is often experienced as the indifference and absence of the faith community. If the pastor, however, is willing to share the functions of ministry with others, seeking out their gifts and equipping them to be effective, then the community's presence is enhanced and genuine pastoral care is much more effective. Not only that, but the wonderful diversity of ways that faith can be expressed is legitimated and becomes a source of growth for the whole congregation.

"Pastor, will you pray for me?" she asked.

"Of course," the pastor replied, "but you know that your prayers are heard by God as much as mine."

"Well, yes, I suppose so," she replied. "It's just that I can't pray well. My prayers don't sound anything like those we pray in church."

"Well," the pastor responded with a laugh, "frankly, mine don't either."

One of the changes in my ministry as the discipleship model began to develop was the decision to use free, spontaneous prayer instead of printed prayers—whether written by others or myself—in public worship, meetings, and other church events. Our team of pastors made the decision collegially not because we thought our spontaneous prayers would be better than the formal prayers in the liturgy or the prayers written by us or others. Rather, it was born out of the conviction that we had, inadvertently, given the wrong message about praying to those who worshiped and worked with us. By praying such eloquent prayers in public, we were telling others, "Unless you pray like this, your prayers are inadequate." With this small change, we began the process of mentoring our people in the practice of prayer— a sure prescription for a power surge in any congregation.

The power of God is not released downward through the church hierarchy. Rather, the power of God is released upward through the people of God when pastors mentor them in the disciplines and practices of the spiritual life.

ENDING CODEPENDENCY

Changes such as this have a cost for both pastors and people. The membership model of the church and the chaplaincy model of ministry create a spiritually unhealthy codependency. The pastor is affirmed by being needed as the spiritual center of the church, and the member feels affirmed by the pastor's attention. A pastor's effectiveness is determined by how much others need him or her. Soon both pastor and congregation begin functioning in ways that create and affirm the cycle of need and response. Breaking these patterns of codependency can be difficult and painful. The pastor's role must be redefined, and the parishioners must become responsible for their own spiritual health.

For "members" of the church within the membership model's patterns of codependency, faith is not costly. Personal spiritual growth is not expected. People are neither responsible nor accountable for their own spiritual journeys. Spiritual disciplines and practices are not encouraged. Should an individual become frustrated with the church and its ministry or feel spiritually empty and "unfed," it is quickly concluded that there must be a problem with the pastor or some other staff member or lay leader. If the pastor or other leader doesn't change and thus "fix the problem," the result is usually outright—or passive-aggressive—conflict, followed by either the capitulation of the pastor or the departure of the member.

Clearly I have painted a stark picture of the roles and relationships that typify a chaplaincy-based ministry. But ask almost any pastor about the dynamics of his or her ministry and these unhealthy relationships will rear their ugly heads. The discipleship model offers a perspective from which we can reevaluate pastoral relationships and the goals of pastoral ministries and then construct new strategies to create healthy relationships and better achieve the ministry goals.

New Expectations
for Pastoral Leadership

"He's a good pastor," the council member told me, "but he can't lead us into a new time of growth. Frankly, his preaching is good, and I understand that he is great on hospital calls. But our young people are leaving—and they aren't coming back! What we need is vision and energy. And he doesn't have either."

The conversation was fairly one-sided. But it is typical of many that I have heard at our Changing Church Conferences, annual gatherings on leadership strategies for churches interested in positive change and growth. Clearly, the stated issue was whether the pastor was doing a good job or not and, perhaps more importantly, whether he was doing the *right* job or not. And clearly the problem lay in the fact that the pastor's understanding of the job description and the council member's understanding were not the same.

The expectations of clergy are dramatically shifting, but few pastors seem to have a clear sense of the new landscape. Many lay leaders are experiencing increasing uneasiness and dissatisfaction with pastoral ministry, yet very few members of church boards and committees are able to clearly articulate why they no may longer experience the pastor they have loved as "doing the job." I believe that congregational expectations of clergy are shifting to include leadership—the ability to lead others both into and in ministry and mission. It is quickly becoming the case that leadership skills are being looked for and evaluated more highly than skills in pastoral care, preaching, or teaching, which are the traditional roles for which our clergy are trained.

The pastor as spiritual leader is emerging as a much more dynamic and effective pastoral role than those of pastor as caregiver, teacher, and preacher. Not the pastor as spiritual *authority,* but as spiritual *leader, guide,* or *mentor,* one who, out of the depths of his or her own spiritual life, can lead others into spiritually grounded lives of discipleship. In this time of changing expectations, few of our lay leaders can clearly articulate this emerging desire for spiritual leadership. Nevertheless, in most of the conversations I have had with lay leaders about their hopes for pastoral ministry, they confirm that spiritual leadership is what they want from their pastors.

The pastor as spiritual leader represents a critical shift in clergy self-perception. At the risk of oversimplifying, it can be said that pastoral ministry has traditionally been understood in terms of *knowing,* which leads to *doing.* Most theological seminaries still train clergy through the university system. They are quite good at passing on tradition as critical thinking and not quite so good at passing on tradition as critical practice. Be that as it may, the assumption behind much of seminary education seems to be that effective, substantive knowing will lead to effective, substantive doing. Unfortunately, it just doesn't work that way.

The pastor as spiritual leader is emerging as a much more dynamic and effective pastoral role than those of pastor as caregiver, teacher, and preacher.

I do not want to disparage theological education. Critical biblical and theological knowledge and skills are essential to confessing and professing the faith and to faithful proclamation and public ministry. As the decline of the mainline churches clearly signals, however, such knowing does not necessarily translate into effecting doing. And even when it does, the "effective doing" is the doing of the pastor. What is needed in today's context are not pastors who "do" ministry but pastors who, from the wellspring of their own spirituality, "lead" others in the doing of ministry.

The pastor as spiritual leader understands her role as grounded in and emerging from her own spiritual center. Her role draws more on wisdom and love than on knowledge. Thus, there is a shift from "knowing leads to *doing*" to "being leads to knowing, which leads to *leading.*"

Leadership is always an *inside-out* affair. A leader's capability to lead is directly related to her inner integrity and character. There have, perhaps, been times when this was not true. But in this age when the skepticism of our followers is the first hurdle of leadership, the inner courage and conviction, the values and beliefs, and the *being* of the leader will be tested again and again.

A spiritual leader recognizes her own need for spiritual strength. The spiritual leader who encourages others to pray must first be a prayerful person. The leader who calls for the service of others in the world must first engage the world in self-giving service. The leader who lifts up the need for spiritual truth in our world must first live in and out of that truth. The leader who would proclaim the word of God, who would effectively bring a word from God into each and every context of contemporary life, must first live deeply in and from the word. This is discipleship. This is authentic Christian spirituality.

DAILY CHOOSING THE WAYS OF GOD

Spirituality is a well-used and abused word in the contemporary religious marketplace. Books, tapes, videos, and seminars on spirituality of one kind or another abound. We find ourselves surrounded by a bewildering variety of "spiritual truths" and techniques, testifying both to the American fascination with the quick and painless fix and the American ability to turn anything into a commodity. The people who sit in church pews on Sunday are not immune to the attractions and influence of the religious marketplace, and strange ideas about spirituality often penetrate the thought and practice of Christian people. This cultural groundswell of interest in spirituality is part of the reason why Christians are looking to their pastors for spiritual leadership.

What is Christian spirituality? In a nutshell, the spiritual life is nothing more—and certainly nothing less—than daily choosing the ways of God, and spirituality is the quality or state of being attuned to the ways of God.[5] Biblically, perhaps the best short definition of Christian spirituality is found in the book of the prophet Micah: "He has told you, O mortal, what is good; and what does the Lord require of you but to do justice, and to love kindness, and to walk humbly with your God?" (Micah 6:8).

Spiritual leadership emerges from the Christian leader's choosing daily the ways of God. Through the personal exercise of the marks of discipleship, the leader grows in wisdom, becoming more and more attuned to the ways of God, more and more able to train others in the marks of discipleship.

Given the finitude and sinfulness of human existence, daily choosing the ways of God is a journey marked by both success and failure. Failure, however, is often the moment of greatest learning. Those spiritual leaders who are engaged by God and then engage the world in mission will be those for whom perfection is not an ideal.

Perfect leaders have no need to be followers. Perfect leaders have no need to be forgiven. In short, perfect leaders have no need for Christ. As Paul proclaimed, "In him we live and move and have our being" (Acts 17:28). Those who experience Christ at the core of their inner life and engage the world with that perspective are not afraid to share their moments of both success and failure, of grace and learning. That is the journey from being to knowing to leading.

True Spiritual Leadership Is Vulnerable and Transparent

I saw him across the parking lot. He smiled and waved, and I continued to walk toward him. I knew him by name and had seen him involved in ministry at our church.

As I neared, he said, "Hi, Pastor Mike. How's your prayer life?"

I responded by greeting him and then, in good pastoral style, said, "My prayer life is fine."

As I continued past him, I realized that I hadn't told him the truth. My prayer life was not fine. I was in a dry spell. My prayers were mostly on the run, and the nearness of God seemed more a memory than an active reality. So I stopped and, turning back to him, said, "I'm sorry. That's not the truth. I'm not doing so well in my prayers. Right now it's hard to pray and God seems distant."

His smile faded. His face fell. After all, it is a difficult thing to hear that your senior pastor's prayer life is not very effective. Then he looked me in the eyes and said, "I'm sorry, Pastor Mike. I'll pray for you."

> **The pastor is first and foremost a disciple in his or her own right.**

The pastor is first and foremost a disciple in his or her own right. Disciples are not perfect—but they keep on following Christ, making up for their own weaknesses with the strengths of others.

One need only remember Peter and his reprimanding of Christ, in Mark 8:27-33, to see how spiritual failure is a natural part of the life of faith. There we see that even after all that personal mentoring by Jesus, the disciples still didn't get it. Yet their leadership would eventually turn the world upside down.

Contemporary Christian leaders must take heart from the experience of the earliest disciples. Leading from the position of one who daily experiences the freedom of divine forgiveness and forbearance enables one to lead without the carping criticism and judgmentalism that sap the enthusiasm and energy of those who follow. Leading from a position of vulnerable and transparent faith means experiencing the highs and lows of the inner life, learning from both, and enabling others to do the same.

What a gift that man in the parking lot gave me. I was not only able to tell him the truth about my spiritual desert, but I also received his understanding and support in return. And I dare to believe that experiences such as this enhance my abilities to lead. Such leadership breaks the patterns of codependency and replaces them with healthy interdependent relationships.

Without the weight of performance anxieties, Christian leaders can focus their ministries on discipleship and mission. Discipleship and mission then become the lenses through which one examines the worship and programs, issues and opportunities, conflicts and achievements of the church. Spiritual leadership within that model expects all decisions to be grounded in prayer and in God's word. Then, with the requirements of discipleship and the mission of the church before us, we dialogue, argue, decide, and act. The question is never whether any particular idea is, in itself, a good idea, nor even if that which is before us is financially doable. The questions we struggle with are never about privilege or power, control or authority. The question is always whether this or that strategy, objective, or activity furthers discipleship and engages us in mission—in God's love for the world.

QUESTIONS FOR PRAYERFUL REFLECTION

1. Is the model of ministry followed in your congregation best described as chaplaincy or spiritual leadership? On what do you base your assessment?

2. If your congregation has a chaplaincy model of ministry and wants to move to the spiritual leadership model, (1) what kind of changes would be necessary, and (2) what kind of resistance could you expect?

3. Are the relationships between pastors and staff and the membership of your congregation best characterized as codependent or interdependent? Why?

4. What problems and possibilities do you see for your congregation in "raising the bar" of expectation to a call for discipleship?

5. What is your definition of spirituality? How does your understanding of spirituality inform your ministry and daily life and relationships?

SPIRITUALITY IS BEING ATTUNED
TO THE WAYS OF GOD.
THE SPIRITUAL LIFE IS
CHOOSING THEM DAILY.

3

six critical marks of leadership

Leadership, like spirituality, is a contemporary buzzword. Everybody uses it, but few agree on what it means. Although there are many different leadership styles—perhaps as many as there are personality types—we nonetheless can identify six critical elements of leadership that are essential in vital discipleship churches.

LEADING FROM FAITH

The first critical element of leadership seems obvious but still needs saying: *pastoral and lay congregational leaders must be persons of faith who are committed to personal discipleship.* This is the sine qua non of Christian leadership.

I have never met a pastor who was called to ministry without having had a significant experience of the presence of God. Nor have I met significant lay leaders who have given time, energy, and passion for the ministry of a congregation who have not first felt the touch of God's love in Jesus Christ. And yet it is often the case that over time the sense of God's presence dims, energy and passion diminish, the fires of the Spirit are quenched, and ministry becomes exhausting rather than enlivening. This is particularly true in the membership model of the church.

The first critical requirement for leadership in our churches is, on the one hand, for present leaders to recapture the spiritual roots of their calling and, on the other hand, to ensure that those who assume new roles of leadership in the church are persons of active faith committed to their own and others' discipleship. In short, the first critical element of Christian leadership is to lead from active, living faith.

SEEING AND CASTING THE VISION

The second critical element of leadership is *the ability to see and to cast the vision*. Vision is not just the picture of the preferred future. It is also the picture of the desired present. Leaders in ministry cast the vision by taking every opportunity to share the picture of the church as they believe it can and should be in the present. In doing so, they must describe in vivid, persuasive, and realistic images what their particular congregation would look like if it were truly, faithfully engaged in the world through a passionate commitment to discipleship and the mission of God's love.

I have come to agree with George Barna that the vision for ministry comes first to the leader.[6] From the soul of the leader will come the vision of possibilities that can capture the hearts and wills of those who follow. This is a "pinpointed passion." It calls forth the highest levels of personal commitment on the part of the leader. If leaders will not risk themselves for the vision, they have no right to ask anyone else to do so. With prayerful seeking and listening to God, the heart of the leader can be stirred to dream a dream that is worthy of his or her best.

CONTEXTUALIZING THE VISION

The third critical element of leadership is *the ability to place the vision firmly and realistically within the community's context.* A vision that is unrelated to the concrete realities and real-life world of the congregation is little more than a pipe dream.

When Pastor Walt Kallestad of Community Church of Joy in Glendale, Arizona, envisioned a ministry that would encompass hundreds of acres, he planted that vision firmly within the local cultural context. In an area of the United States where one in ten worship on any given Sunday, his vision of a Christian missional community that would serve as a training center for Christians as well as an enclave of faith within the secular desert makes a great deal of sense. From senior housing to a water park, from a child-care center to a Christian college, his vision matches the mission field in which God has planted him. And even its grandiose size fits the context. In the sprawling Southwest, this expansive mission outpost for the Christian church seeks to call to Jesus Christ all those outside the faith.

No matter what a leader's vision might be, it must be capable of being incarnated in a particular context. For some, that context will be the inner city with its peculiar realities. For others, it will be the suburbs with their unique issues. And for still others, it will be rural America with its pressing problems. Whatever the setting, the job of leaders is to share the vision for ministry by placing it firmly within their community context.

This can be done in a number of ways. Most importantly, leaders must immerse themselves in their community—get to know it, identify with it, love it. Only from this vantage point will prayer produce a workable, contextualized vision. Once the vision is written out, it must be shared with a called group of constituents within the congregation, including its leadership circle. Pray together. Read an appropriate scripture and share about it. Then, in humility, subject the vision to this group. These men and women live in the larger community; they know it, care about it, and are positioned to know whether the vision is indeed relevant to the social, cultural, and geographical context.

> **Leaders must immerse themselves in their community—get to know it, identify with it, love it.**

At Prince of Peace, we identified 240 ministry leaders to whom we sent an invitation to come to an initial information meeting. We asked the 90 or so who came to prayerfully listen to the charge before us and then prayerfully reflect on whether God was calling them to participate in an intensive process designed to define the vision for our ministry. The key was for them to determine through prayer and consideration whether they were being called by Christ to participate. More than 40 individuals agreed to a yearlong process of study, conversation, and vision seeking.

First we learned together of our internal and external context. We took a "snapshot" of our current situation to get the real picture of our congregation and its ministry. We determined the geographical area where we actually served and where we felt called to serve and examined its demographic mix. What were the income and household profiles of those in the ministry area we sought to serve? Of those in the area we presently served? These and other pieces of crucial information are available through critical surveys of one's own congregation as well as through the services of groups such as *Percept,* an organization that creates "ministry area profiles" on the basis of careful demographic research.[7]

Once we felt confident that we knew our context, I prayerfully dreamed a dream for our ministry together. After writing it down, I shared it with our group. I admit that I was anxious: what would I do if they didn't buy it? Couldn't see it? Rejected it? But there was no need for anxiety. I spoke, and they listened respectfully and then got down to the task of refining the vision.

The casting of a vision is not unlike giving birth. The leader conceives the vision, and the community, through its leaders, acts as midwife in its birth. Once the vision has come to life, it takes on an existence of its own. Thus, vision casting is a dynamic process between those who lead and those who follow. No vision can be sufficiently compelling without everyone playing their parts. The passion of the vision demands ownership by the community, and clarity of vision is achieved when the leader entrusts it to the whole community. When this happens, the vision becomes a beacon, guiding the congregation through the rough waters of conflict and change.

ALIGNING THE CONGREGATION TO THE VISION

Many a worthy vision has failed because either the rank and file didn't own it or the internal systems of the congregation worked against it. The fourth critical element for leadership, therefore, is *the ability to enroll the constituency and align the institutional structures of the congregation to the vision.*

Once it became clear that my vision for ministry required a shift from the membership model to the discipleship model, it was clear that the congregation had to own the vision and fundamental organizational changes had to be implemented in the church. Since I believe that all leaders lead, it was crucial that the staff and church council members accept, endorse, and live the vision.

I arranged one-on-one meetings with each of the council members. We walked through the "marks of discipleship," core values for our unfolding vision. I explained that disciples are those who make a personal commitment to spiritual growth by striving to (1) pray daily, (2) worship weekly, (3) read the Bible, (4) serve others both at and beyond Prince of Peace, (5) encourage spiritual growth in others through their relationships, and (6) give freely of their time, talents, and resources.

I asked for their opinions and concerns about this list of expectations for leaders. I told them I was convinced that the viability of our ministry was directly related to our willingness to move from being a "low expectation" church to a "high expectation" one. I told them that leaders would not only have to agree with this premise, but also strive to practice the marks of discipleship.

One council member looked at the expectation to worship weekly and asked, "Does this mean I'll have to sell my lake cabin?"

"No," I replied. "It means that just because you are at the lake, your need to worship is not gone. Have family devotions or, better yet, if there is a church nearby, worship there."

He smiled and said, "Well, there is this small church just down the road from our place, and we've been talking about going there. I guess now we will."

After the council members expressed their willingness to both support and live the discipleship model, I met with the entire staff. I shared with each one the vision for a ministry based on discipleship. Then I told them that the basis for our ministry together had changed. If any of us lacked particular skills for ministry, we could learn them. Spiritual integrity, however, was an up-front requirement for working as a part of our staff.

Every staff member, regardless of her or his position, was a minister. Thus, any visitor should be able to ask any staff member about our programmatic ministries and the faith, values, and convictions that undergird them and receive a helpful and accurate picture of our community of faith. Every staff member was to understand her or his role as that of a spiritual leader.

Each staff member was invited into conversation about the marks of discipleship as biblical and traditional practices of the faith. Then each was asked to endorse and practice them to the best of their ability. One staff member looked at me somewhat incredulously and asked, "Does this mean that if I'm reading my Bible and praying in my office,

> Every staff member was to understand her or his role as that of a spiritual leader.

no one will come and tell me I'm not doing my job?"

"That's exactly what it means," I replied. "In fact, the most important thing you can do for your work is to practice your faith on a daily basis here. I'm convinced that your work will become better focused and you will actually accomplish more because of it."

My goal was not only to enroll the council members and the staff in the discipleship vision, but to ask them to align their personal lives and work with it as well. Now we have regular prayer and Bible study as part of our staff meetings and ministry team meetings. Board members bring their Bibles to meetings expecting time for both Bible study and common prayer with one another. Members of our facilities service team regularly pray for those who will walk the floors of the church they are washing.

The next step was to achieve broad congregational awareness of our commitment to discipleship and to invite our lay ministry leaders to also adopt the marks of discipleship. This process continues. Originally I assumed that this would take at least five years to accomplish. That was an optimistic assessment. Changing the culture of a large organization through the power of a new vision is a slow and challenging task. But it is transforming in its outcome—and more than worth the effort!

CONTINUALLY COMMUNICATING THE VISION

The fifth critical element of leadership is *the will to keep creatively repeating the vision and inspiring those who follow to embrace it.* I've learned from experience the simple truth that you cannot over-communicate the vision of a changing church. The tragedy, as John Kotter points out, is that leaders all too frequently under-communicate the vision.

> A great vision can serve a useful purpose even if it is understood by just a few key people. But the real power of a vision is unleashed only when most of those involved in an enterprise or activity have a common understanding of its goals and directions. . . . Gaining understanding and commitment to a new direction is never an easy task, especially in large enterprises. Smart people make mistakes here all the time, and outright failure is not uncommon. . . . Managers under-communicate and often not by a small amount.[8]

Frequently those in leadership communicate their vision by preaching a sermon or two on the topic, writing an article for the parish newsletter, and leading a special class or "town meeting." They then assume that those they seek to influence have fully understood the vision. But it doesn't happen that way.

As our congregation began the move toward the discipleship model, I preached a series of sermons on the marks of discipleship and the following year preached another series of sermons that referenced the marks. Then we surveyed the members of our New Disciples Class and discovered that they were still unclear as to what the marks of discipleship were and what they meant for our congregation. These were the people who ought to have been most clear on them! I suspect that Kotter is right and that I have under-communicated the vision and the practices of that vision by a factor of ten.

My visit to the DreamWorks studio in Hollywood drove home the point. At the time they were in production of their first full-length animated feature, *The Prince of Egypt*. As we entered the studio, we passed by the storyboard of the film. Absolutely no one working on the project could enter or leave that studio without being reminded of why they were there and what they were about. Whether it was one of the principles of the organization or a food service worker in the cafeteria, each had her or his activities directly linked to the mission and vision of the feature animation. The power of purpose was palpable in that setting, and I believe it was directly linked to the clear and repeated vision that guided each employee's work.

I again saw the power of repeated vision and mission while at the Disney Institute in Orlando, Florida. Between sessions, a friend took me to the door of a storeroom labeled "Cast Only." That in itself was a surprise. I discovered that Disney does not have employees. All are "cast members," whose roles support the creation of a great experience for those who visit the theme park. Opening the door, my friend pointed to a simple sign that every cast member who entered or left that storeroom had to pass by. The sign read, "Remember hospitality counts! Watch your body language." And beneath that reminder was a picture of a water-skier waving and obviously having great fun. The message was simple yet profound. Cast members needed to understand that they were all gracious hosts, no matter what their individual role might be. And they ought to have great fun doing it!

We need similar strategies to keep the vision continually in front of our people, to continually communicate what we are about and why we are about it and to inspire people to be a part of it. Could there be storyboards in our congregations reminding us all of why we come to church and why we go back out into the world? I have heard of a church with a sign reading "Servant's Entrance" over the door leading out of the church. It reminds everyone of who they are and to what mission they are called. Could usher closets have notices like the one in the storerooms at Disney World? Just as Disney World communicates over and over that it has no employees, only "cast members," how do we communicate that we have no members, only "disciples"?

> **We must plant the vision deep in the heart of the mission of the church and deep in the hearts of those who come to church.**

Simply communicating the vision once, twice, or even thrice is not enough. We must plant the vision deep in the heart of the mission of the church and deep in the hearts of those who come to church. That is to say, we must weave it into the very fabric of our self-understanding as Christians. Purpose breeds personal power. The purpose of the Christian church—"faith active in love"—when connected to the lives of individual and family disciples is incredibly empowering.

Change Management

The sixth and last critical element of leadership is *the ability to manage change.* The realization of vision requires change. Change begun and not well managed will, on the one hand, fail and, on the other hand, hurt the congregation and those who care about it.

In a parable that Jesus told, he described the kingdom as "like yeast that a woman took and mixed in with three measures of flour until all of it was leavened" (Matthew 13:33). Change is like yeast. The first step—call it opening the package of yeast—is the official adoption of the change. Next the change needs to be introduced throughout all levels of the organization—worked like yeast into the flour. This allows the change to penetrate throughout the various areas of ministry where it will begin to move each individual ministry toward realization of the common vision. Once a given change has been introduced into the many areas of ministry where its influence must be felt, it takes on a life of its own—just like yeast. With consistency of purpose and performance, change will work.

The role of leadership is to communicate the necessity of change, interpret its impact and consequences, listen to positive feedback, make adjustments where experience indicates the need, and recognize, celebrate, and reward successful implementation. Change is experienced most acutely by two kinds of people: those directly responsible for its implementation and those who most directly feel its consequences. The leader manages the experiences of both by clarifying the needs for the change, being open about its costs and benefits, and demonstrating how it will help the organization better achieve its mission and vision.

Also crucial to managing change is the insistence upon continued implementation. This is the hard work of discipline.

So many changes have been subverted by leaders who initiate the change and then wrongly assume that it will naturally happen. John Kotter, in his significant book *Leading Change*, identifies the following necessary steps for the effective management of change:

- Establishing a sense of urgency
- Creating a guiding coalition
- Developing a vision and strategy
- Communicating the change vision
- Empowering employees for broad-based action
- Generating short-term wins
- Consolidating gains and producing more change
- Anchoring new approaches in the culture[9]

Careful attention to these eight steps establishes the climate for successful change.

Effective management of change is essential if congregations are to grow into a viable and faithful future. Such work requires both commitment and discipline on the part of the leader and the leadership team. The natural resistance to change does not go away simply because change has been introduced. When leaders work the change into the system, however, like a baker kneading yeast into dough, the impact is profound: lively growth!

QUESTIONS FOR PRAYERFUL REFLECTION

1. Carefully reflect on the six critical marks of leadership and check which are your areas of strength and which are your areas of growth:

	Strength	Growth
Commitment to personal discipleship	_____	_____
Ability to see and cast the vision	_____	_____
Ability to contextualize the vision	_____	_____
Ability to align community and vision	_____	_____
Ability to continually communicate	_____	_____
Ability to manage change	_____	_____

2. To change any of these from areas of growth to areas of strength, what would you need to do? With whom would you need to do it?

3. Can you identify a group of lay leaders in your congregation who could engage in a visioning process like the one described in this chapter?

4. How does your community of faith react to change?

5. What might you do to help the community react more positively to change?

WITH CONSISTENCY OF PURPOSE AND PERFORMANCE, POSITIVE CHANGE HAPPENS.

4 culture shock!

When congregational change is as fundamental as a paradigm shift—such as the church's move from a membership model to a discipleship model—the congregational culture is in for a shock. A big shock! The entire shape of the congregation is at stake. Both the form and the function of the community of faith will be impacted. The cost is great—but the benefits are huge.

When we implemented the marks of discipleship at Prince of Peace, I knew that getting verbal agreement to the goal of discipleship as well as to the value of the practices was the first, and perhaps easiest, step in what would be a long process of change. Since then, we have been actively integrating the marks of discipleship into every aspect of our ministry—with growing success.

New Roles and New Responsibilities for Everyone

The integration of the discipleship model into the life of the congregation has not been without cost. One of the major costs has been the inevitable realignment of roles and responsibilities. The membership model's clarity of roles and structure provided security for leadership and membership alike. The members knew that their job was to take care of the "business" of the church while the pastor (and staff) took care of everyone's spiritual needs. When all are disciples, however, that clarity of role is quickly blurred.

As most pastors are aware, the church is replete with individuals who, with proper mentoring, are quite able to participate powerfully both in the spiritual life of the community of faith and in the mission of the church to the larger world. Indeed, it is often the case that some members of the community of faith may well have gifts that the pastor does not. For example, some pastors are incredibly gifted at hospital calling and visiting the homebound and those in nursing homes. Others are not. The old ministry model prescribed such pastoral visits as a central activity for clergy—whether they were good at it or not. Worse yet, it either precluded gifted laity from such activities or relegated their visiting to second-class status, even if they had a first-class gift.

Getting used to the new alignments of roles and responsibilities required by the discipleship model is admittedly difficult. The congregational culture is shocked, and people feel a sense of dislocation. Pastors may understandably begin to feel marginalized and threatened when they discover that areas of ministry that have been expected of them in the past can actually be done better by others. Lay disciples may feel insecure and uneasy—if not inappropriate!—as they step across boundaries into areas of ministry that have been largely reserved for pastors. All need to be reminded repeatedly that discipleship is a matter of calling, giftedness, and training—not title or position.

ONENESS WITH CHRIST AND WITH ONE ANOTHER IN CHRIST

The benefit to paying the price for moving from membership to discipleship is a power surge for the congregation—the release of the Spirit of Jesus Christ. Adults and children discover the depth and breadth of their oneness with Christ and their oneness in Christ with each other, and the result is new energy and passion, a new sense of joy and meaning, and a church marked by healthy interdependence rather than codependence.

In both Romans and 1 Corinthians, Paul reminds us that all of God's people are gifted people: "For as in one body we have many members, and not all the members have the same function, so we, who are many, are one body in Christ, and individually we are members one of another. We have gifts that differ according to the grace given to us" (Romans 12:4-6; cf. 1 Corinthians 12:4-31).

Most churches pay lip service to the Pauline imagery of the multigifted body of Christ, but it is time to do more than that. It is time to take the imagery with literal seriousness. The discipleship model of the church is gift-based. It believes not only that the Spirit has given gifts to God's people, but that in the exercise of those gifts for the common good, God's people experience the abundant life that Jesus proclaimed.

> All need to be reminded repeatedly that discipleship is a matter of calling, giftedness, and training—not title or position.

The discipleship model does not use guilt or coercion to engage people in the work of the church. Rather, it proclaims the promises of Christ and encourages people to be who they are in response to the call of Christ. "*You will* receive power when the Holy Spirit has come *upon you;* and *you will* be my witnesses . . . to the ends of the earth" (Acts 1:8, emphasis added; cf. 2:38-39).

The membership model stifles the gifts of God's people and pigeonholes the "members" into roles that may not suit their gifts at all. Any church that takes seriously the Spirit-given gifts of its people and both encourages and enables their use as a matter of faithful discipleship will thrive in the twenty-first century. Those that do not will struggle and die.

STEPPING BACK FROM CONTROL

"Pastor," she said, "we have asked you to be here because we believe God is leading us into a time of great prayer."

I wondered what was coming and what it would mean for my busy schedule. She continued.

"We have been longing for years for the spiritual renewal of this church. And we know it must begin with our leaders— that means our staff. So we are offering ourselves to pray for and with the staff. We'd like to offer centering prayer as the model,[10] but we know that we need your support in order to do this. We want to do it so that we can fill you up—fill the staff through the gift of prayer."

It was a great idea, but as I listened to her, I was thinking, "One more thing to get ready for!" She continued.

"And we don't want the staff to have to do any preparation. So we'll come and lead the prayers. We'll also choose appropriate Bible verses for reading. We'll arrange everything. We just need you to set a convenient time and place."

For a senior pastor—particularly one trained in the chaplaincy model of ministry—it's not easy to be asked to step back from leading the prayers and devotions of your key staff leaders. But it was time to "walk the talk." As a congregation, we had committed ourselves to discipleship. We affirmed the call of disciples of Christ who hear the voice of God and seek to obey it in ways that are consistent with our mission and vision. There was no getting away from it.

"It is always a scary thing to be taken seriously," I said. As we laughed together, I knew that stepping back was required of me.

Stepping back does not mean relinquishing appropriate control. It does mean striving to assess whether and to what degree any control is necessary. Nor does it mean anything goes. Spiritual leadership under the discipleship model takes very seriously the role and responsibility of mentoring the disciples of Christ in the effective use of their gifts. There are no easy answers here. Stepping back is a dance, not a blueprint. It is, however, the wonderful dance of the Holy Spirit released in the lives of God's faithful people.

Stepping back requires the leadership of the congregation to see more and do less. From their informed vantage point, leaders need to ask the strategic questions that ensure consistency of purpose and performance in ministry and mission. Does the suggested ministry, program, or activity fit the context? Is there a match with our common understanding of who we are and what we are called to be and do? Is now the best time for this activity? Will it add to our momentum and advance us toward our vision, or will it distract us and get us moving in the wrong direction? How might it be implemented, by whom, and with what resources? Are the resources available, and would this be the best use of our resources at this time?

As I listened to those wonderful disciples called to and gifted in prayer ministry, those were the kinds of questions I pondered. The result was the creating of a strategic prayer ministry that first involved the staff and then moved into the entire congregation. The ultimate goal was to deepen the faith life of the whole church—not just support the staff. That fit our mission and vision!

In this case, I was asked to "see more" by listening to the prompting of the Spirit in the lives of others. Prayer connects us to the Infinite and thus opens up infinite possibilities. Their vision was not mine, but for the sake of the church, the implementation of it required my involvement. My task was both to see their vision and then to see how it fit in the life of the whole church.

The wonderful thing about it all was that they were asking me to do less. I was no longer solely responsible for filling the staff—or the congregation—through prayer. These faithful disciples of Christ had the gift, heard the call, and were willing to step forward and serve God's people in a new and exciting ministry of prayer.

CLARIFYING EXPECTATIONS

To survive the culture shock of a paradigm shift and successfully traverse the terrain of a new model of the church, spiritual leadership must continuously clarify—through both word and example—the expectations for the community. If the church is to be based on discipleship, leaders must live the marks of discipleship and help to create a culture of mutual accountability. Leaders of a discipleship church must embody the new culture. Their words and actions clarify, teach, and reinforce the expectations, behaviors, values, beliefs, and hopes of the discipleship model.

Let us be clear. This is not a call to perfection. Even a cursory reading of the New Testament leaves no doubt that the first disciples of Christ were anything but perfect. But they were willing to learn. They failed and were forgiven; they misunderstood and then sought understanding; they gave in to weakness and fear, then sought to encourage one another; they ran from discipleship and then returned to the one who had called them.

In a discipleship church, human weaknesses and failings are simply opportunities to learn—and to teach—forgiveness. Modeling discipleship means being honest and transparent about one's own life of faith, admitting difficulties where they exist, owning up to mistakes, and making amends—but never as failure! In a discipleship church, *failure is not failure if we learn from it,* grow from it, and change as a result of it.

The culture of a discipleship church is a culture of forgiveness. Disciples embrace and seek to follow the profound teaching of Ephesians: "Be kind to one another, tenderhearted, forgiving one another, as God in Christ has forgiven you. Therefore be imitators of God, as beloved children, and live in love, as Christ loved us" (Ephesians 4:32–5:1). Clarifying, teaching, modeling, and reinforcing the expectations of discipleship can only be done upon this bedrock of grace. God's love is the context within which disciples live, serve, sin, and grow.

THE JOY OF UNCONDITIONAL GRACE

The joy of discipleship begins here, in the experience of unconditional grace. The membership model had shifted ministry's center to the member. Mission had been pushed to the margins and Christ was often reduced to little more than an interesting historical figure. Discipleship, however, recenters mission as the heart of the church and reconnects believers to a living, always present Christ: Christ, the one who loves unconditionally yet holds us accountable to his love; Christ, the one who unconditionally forgives but uses the consequences of sin to shape character; Christ, the one who is present and active every day, calling God's people to purpose and community.

Reconnected to the living Christ, disciples are open to interdependency. Personal inadequacies are not failures so much as opportunities to discover the gifts of others. Community is not simply shared identity. It is the result of shared labor toward common goals. The joy of interdependence is in the experience that the whole truly is greater than the individual parts. When we all work together using our individual gifts for the common good, we are all better than we could possibly be alone.

> Community is not simply shared identity. It is the result of shared labor toward common goals.

The way to set people free to use their gifts is simply to set them free! Discipleship church leaders create space for people to learn by doing. Doing is not simply about making something happen. Doing itself is about learning. The only way to be a disciple is to become a disciple by doing the things a disciple does and learning from the experience. A congregational culture that identifies, validates, encourages, publicly recognizes, trains, and uses the Spirit-given gifts of its people will experience incredible power surges. That's real culture shock!

In such a gift-based culture as one finds in the discipleship model, people are willing to risk themselves without fear. Their willingness to risk leads the church into innovation. That innovation is used by the Spirit to create useful change and advance Christ's reign. The only caveat is that we be willing to hold ourselves accountable to the mission of God and the vision of the congregation as well as to an honest assessment of our gifts.

Every year Prince of Peace has a Mega-Garage Sale. It was not my idea! In fact, to be honest, I don't like garage sales of any size. But this garage sale is totally dedicated to charity. Fifty percent of the net proceeds go outside of Prince of Peace, and 50 percent go to ministries within Prince of Peace, with none of the proceeds going to the women's ministry that sponsors the sale. Last year, more than $60,000 was given away. No wonder it keeps growing!

The focus of the women who give of their gifts, time, and energy for the garage sale is on mission, not on themselves. The joy they feel when they prayerfully make the decisions of where all the money will go is phenomenal.

The first to go through the Mega-Garage Sale are families identified through social service agencies as in dire need. They take what they need for free. Then the sale is held, and when it is over, whatever has not been sold is given to a Hmong group who repairs, reconditions, and uses everything. From start to finish, this garage sale is dedicated to the welfare of others.

The power of the garage sale is found in our common commitment to mission. The most I do is help collect furniture and perhaps make a few small purchases. But others give days and days of their time, energy, and love. We have discovered that when the disciples of Jesus are able to connect their gifts and passions to concrete acts of mission, they give far more time and energy than we could have imagined. The garage sale is a small but significant response to God's call to all of us to live beyond ourselves, to be a community in the service of others in the name of Jesus Christ. It is an example of doing justice, loving kindness, and walking humbly with God—living the prophet Micah's marks of the spiritual life.

Such activities not only build identity as disciples, they also build trusting relationships. When we are working with one another for a goal beyond ourselves, we learn to trust one another. Trust is an essential element in healthy interdependency. As we work together we discover our mutual strengths and limitations. We learn that we need each other, that together we are more than we are alone. We learn that in the providence of God we complete each other, and we learn to let go, to let others be for us and with us. Discipleship is a thoroughly relational enterprise. To become a disciple is to become deeply connected—to God and through God to the world God loves. It is an experience of grace and joy.

In the community of faith, learning to trust others is a matter of learning to trust God. Finally (although we often act otherwise), it is God's church, and the wonderful diversity of people that fill the church are also God's—God's gifts to us and God's instruments in the ministry and mission of the church. The joy of discipleship is here, in a faithful, grace-full community where we care and are cared for by God and by one another.

CULTURAL CLUES

If you have ever traveled to a foreign country, you know what culture shock is all about. People do familiar things differently and do some things that simply aren't done "at home." You encounter new and strange habits, customs, and rituals. It takes a while to figure out the "cultural clues" that tell you how to behave in ways that fit with the new culture. Those who make the move from a membership church to a discipleship church are entering a new culture. They need to know a few cultural clues to start feeling at home.

The key to understanding the culture of a discipleship congregation is found in the fact that those who accept the call to discipleship are committed to the personal practice of their own faith. Daily Bible reading is the first cultural clue. *Lectio Divina,* or holy reading, reading the Bible slowly prayerfully, and lovingly, is a mark of discipleship. When we expose ourselves to God's Word, the Holy Spirit has access to our hearts in a remarkable way. Our hearts are shaped by the living Word. Our minds are formed and informed by the truths of God. Our souls are nurtured from the eternal well of God's love. Disciples are those who learn to live in and out of the Word of God. Bibles do not rest on bookshelves and dust does not rest on Bibles in a discipleship church.

The second cultural clue for those entering a discipleship culture is the prevalence of prayer. To speak of daily prayer is perhaps misleading. Life itself becomes prayer for those who live life consciously in relationship with God. Particular times of focused prayer, ongoing conversations with God throughout the day, moments of silence to be still before God and listen—these are common habits of disciples.

In a discipleship culture, people expect to bring prayer into the decision-making process, be it individual or communal decision making. The personal decisions that we make each day—decisions as to how we spend our money, how we spend our time, how we structure our relationships, how we do our jobs, where we get our pleasures, and the like—are informed by the presence of God experienced through both prayer and a prayerful encounter with God's word. And it is the same with the corporate decisions of the community of faith. Discipleship congregations learn to "be still and know that God is God" (Psalm 46:10). They learn to search the mind of God by applying God's word to the realities of their life together, by waiting for God, by listening for the voice of the Spirit that guides the church. It is by community prayer and Bible study around the vision, ministry, and mission of the church that disciples follow Paul's advice in Romans 12:2: "Do not be conformed to this world, but be transformed by the renewing of your minds, so that you may discern what is the will of God—what is good and acceptable and perfect." When you notice people dealing with the concrete realities of their lives through the practices of prayer and holy reading, it is a clue you have entered a culture of discipleship. To live in that culture is to learn to do the same. It is to walk humbly with your God, the third mark, we've already noted, of the spiritual life according to the prophet Micah.

Judging the Thoughts and Intentions of the Heart

The daily practice of faith through the discipline of Bible study and prayer has a way of working on us. The writer of Hebrews put it well: "Indeed, the word of God is living and active, sharper than any two-edged sword . . . ; it is able to judge the thoughts and intentions of the heart" (Hebrews 4:12). The openness to the transforming power of God that disciples bring to the practice of their faith leads to personal growth, increased wholeness, and a deeper experience of joyful living.

"You have to talk to her," that still, small voice demanded. "And do it soon."

Well, I didn't want to. I had spoken ill of her. I had overheard her saying something that I took to be critical of me, and I had been stung. I was hurt by it and perhaps a bit angry. I told another person about it and wondered out loud how she could possibly be a leader in the church.

In prayer, however, I realized that I didn't really know for certain that what she said had been directed at me. And it could have been said—and most likely had been said—without any malicious intent at all.

In the Bible, I read Jesus' teaching: "So when you are offering your gift at the altar, if you remember that your brother or sister has something against you, leave your gift there before the altar and go; first be reconciled to your brother or sister, and then come and offer your gift" (Matthew 5:23-24). The meaning seemed clear: God is far more interested in the health of our relationships than in our religiosity.

What would I do? What would I do not with what she had said, but with what I had said?

I called my friend. I shared my hurt at what had been said and apologized for having complained to others about her. Then I asked for her forgiveness. There was a long pause and she finally said, "Of course you have my forgiveness. But you know, I don't think that conversation had anything to do with you!"

Sometimes—as in this story—our egos get in the way, and we need to let prayer and Bible study do their work in us and through us. This holy work of the Spirit—active through prayer and a deep reflective study of the Bible—holds our ego needs in check and leads us to a healthy humility.

IDENTIFYING THE GIFTS OF GOD'S PEOPLE

The humility arrived at through prayer and a meditative study of the Bible gives us a perspective from which we can more easily identify those around us who have particular gifts for particular ministries or leadership roles. Identifying the gifts of the gifted is essential for moving a congregation from membership to discipleship. It's a part of the culture—identifying, affirming, encouraging, and mentoring. Discovering the gifts of the gifted, however, is a bit like looking for a treasure in an antique mall. We can easily be overwhelmed, not seeing the trees for the forest. A gift assessment tool can help.

At Prince of Peace we use *Life Keys.*[11] This work uses a number of personal assessment tools, including a spiritual gifts inventory and the Myers-Briggs Type Indicator for discerning personality types. Whatever tools you might choose—and there are many—it is wise to develop a congregational priority and strategy for identifying the gifts of God's people in your community of faith. The more we learn about ourselves and about those with whom we serve, the better able we will be to match personal gifts with community roles and activities.

Disciples, of course, live in the world as well as in the church. Faithful discipleship in all the places we live and work and play is also enhanced through the increased self-understanding and appreciation of our particular skills, interests, passions, work, and relational styles, an understanding and appreciation that come from a careful use of gift and personality assessment tools.

GOOD LEADERS DEVELOP LEADERS

John Maxwell has written:

> Those who believe in our ability do more than stimulate us—they create an atmosphere in which it becomes easier for us to succeed. Creating an environment that will attract leaders is vital to any organization. Doing that is the job of leaders.[12]

And according to Noel M. Tichy:

> The essence of winning leadership [is] building into the future by developing the abilities of others. . . . Winning companies win because they have good leaders who nurture the development of other leaders at all levels of the organization.[13]

There are many ways to develop leaders and many leadership styles. The literature on leadership and leadership development is voluminous—and growing daily. Much of it is excellent, and leaders who are serious about bringing out the best in the people who follow them should keep abreast of what's being written. One thing is clear: there is no single developmental approach for every potential leader. Leaders who are serious about growing new leaders for their organizations need to be sensitive to—and appreciative of—the individuality of the people with whom they work.

Metaphorically, we could call leadership development a dance, one where those who lead need to hear and be sensitive to the music that moves those who follow. The metaphor implies that leadership development is not a linear process from objective to goal. Rather, dancing implies a circular or spiraling motion determined by the direction of the music and the sheer joy of moving with it. And dancing implies gaining skill and ever-greater freedom of movement through the discipline of practice.

The dynamics of leadership development include managing, coaching, and watching. Managing means hands-on interaction. It means getting potential leaders involved in ministry from the bottom up. One who has never danced cannot teach dancing. One who has never played baseball cannot manage a team. One who has never worked with youth cannot lead a youth program. If they are eventually going to lead others in ministry, potential leaders need to get their hands dirty, as it were, doing the work of ministry.

Leadership skills, of course, are transferable. Those who hold leadership responsibilities in their vocations will rise to leadership in a discipleship church more quickly than those who don't. Be that as it may, experiencing ministry and mission "close to the ground" is foundational for developing leaders.

Managing leadership development, then, involves engaging potential leaders in grassroots ministry under your—or another's—leadership and then providing opportunities for them to grow. On-the-job-training that grows skills and incrementally adds leadership responsibilities gives potential leaders ministry "feet" to stand on.

The more confident emerging leaders become, the more frequently they will seek coaching rather than managing. Coaching involves helping the developing leader to set boundaries, identify goals and objectives, determine accountability structures, and set benchmarks for evaluation. Then the emerging leader is turned loose to "play the leadership game."

Coaching will finally become more and more passive and evolve into watching or observing. Watching means supporting and, when asked, offering counsel, making suggestions, and giving encouragement. The culture of discipleship discourages micromanagement. Leaders are identified, trained, given the resources for success, and then authorized to do their work. The dance of developing leaders turns people loose as equipped and confident leaders in their own right. It can be a case of real culture shock for those used to a chaplaincy model of ministry where the doing of ministry belongs to the minister and not these developing leaders.

DECENTRALIZING PASTORAL CARE

Tooling up for the discipleship model also means creating an intentional community of care and hospitality. As Dr. Carl George has pointed out, "The chaplaincy model of ministry where the pastors are the only ones who provide pastoral support is dispensing pastoral care by the dropper full."[14] He is absolutely right, and an effective, discipleship-based alternative is to build a community of faith characterized by a common commitment to hospitality and care. Again, this is a matter of organizational culture.

How do you change the atmosphere in a congregation so that the air people breathe is scented with the fragrance of genuine hospitality and compassionate caring? One obvious place to begin is with the spoken and written word. Sermons, newsletter articles, and the like that intentionally focus on the biblical basis for hospitality, for welcoming strangers, for weeping with those who weep and rejoicing with those who rejoice, create expectations within the community. Stories that acknowledge and celebrate real-life instances of unabashed hospitality, gentleness, and compassion reinforce and reward those expectations.

Recall the story in chapter 2 about my early morning trip to the hospital on a pastoral care call. When I arrived at Shirley's room in the hospital, I found a beautiful picture of community care. Instead of having only one pastor to visit and provide support, Shirley had a network of Christian friends that provided a safety net of prayer and a ministry of presence. The church was present, the Body of Christ was present, even when the pastor wasn't. Such stories, when told and celebrated, create a change in the climate, a change

> The expectation that you will be cared for and that you will be called upon to care for others is a clue that you are in a discipleship congregation.

in the culture. The expectation that you will be cared for and that you will be called upon to care for others is a clue that you are in a discipleship congregation.

I have reminded the disciples at Prince of Peace that there will never be enough financial resources to provide adequate pastoral care coverage by clergy. Nor should there be. The stories of small groups and ministry teams caring for their members with spiritual, emotional, and—when needed—material support is both heartwarming and typical of discipleship congregations. The telling of such stories anchors the expectations of discipleship in the community of faith. Ensuring that the stories are told and celebrated in all the places where people gather to worship and work is one way of ensuring that you will never run out of stories to tell. It is also a way to ensure that far more people will be genuinely cared for than could ever be touched directly by the ministry of pastors and staff.

Also, it is vital to implement a clear strategy for equipping people to serve in pastoral care ministries. Extend the call to those who are gifted and train them for service. Provide training opportunities and structured programs for service such as the Stephen Ministers program or the Befrienders program. Resist the notion that you are somehow making "small clergy" out of such caregivers. These are not elitist programs. The fact of the matter is that disciples nurture and care for one another and such programs provide opportunities for ordinary disciples to develop and hone skills that enable them to be a caring presence wherever they might find themselves.

Much of the hospitality and caring that take place in a discipleship congregation happens in small group settings. As people get to know each other and are encouraged to actively care for each other, remarkable things happen. When, in the context of faith, people learn to be truly present to each other, to be open and vulnerable with each other, they become, to borrow Martin Luther's expression, Christs to each other.

> Hence, as our heavenly Father has in Christ freely come to our aid, we also ought to freely help our neighbor through our body and its works, and each one should become as it were a Christ to the other that we may be Christs to one another and Christ may be the same in all, that is, that we may be truly Christian.[15]

To be "truly Christian" is to be truly hospitable and caring as Christ was and, in so doing, to make Christ truly present in the community of faith and in the larger community outside the church.

It is vital for the spiritual leadership of a discipleship congregation to plant a theology of hospitality and care in every small group, every ministry team, every event, and every program of the church. The spiritual leadership of the congregation must embody and live out a theology of hospitality and care. The expectation should be clear: disciples take care of each other. It is another cultural clue.

A caring culture quite naturally has a strong commitment to hospitality. "Faith active in love," the purpose of the church, demands it. A significant moment in the maturing of the first church centered around the issue of hospitality. With the press of evangelistic need, the disciples were harried, pressed for time, and under the tyranny of the urgent, were neglecting the material needs of the weaker members of the community. For instance, the book of Acts records that "during those days, when the disciples were increasing in number, the Hellenists complained against the Hebrews because their widows were being neglected in the daily distribution of food" (Acts 6:1).

> It is vital for the spiritual leadership of a discipleship congregation to plant a theology of hospitality and care.

In response to the complaint, the church established the office of deacon and appointed seven men to the task of seeing that people's needs were tended to. It was arguably the first organized hospitality ministry!

Hospitality opens the door to care. The climate of any community of faith is experienced as hot or cold, caring or distant through the presence or lack of heartfelt hospitality. A community of care recognizes the clear call of God that

Christ's church reach out to the sojourner and stranger. How we greet people sets the stage for how we shall both care for them and ultimately engage them in caring for others. Disciples understand the expectation that we shall be a caring community within and beyond our immediate circle. This is not an either-or. It is a both-and of the Gospel.

THE DIVINE CONNECTION

"I didn't want to join a large church," he said. "I just didn't think that a large church could provide the stuff I needed. But I kept coming back." He chuckled as he continued. "I tried most of the other smaller churches in the area. I'd go to Prince of Peace one weekend and then a smaller church the next. But, somehow, I felt like I met God in worship here." He paused. "It's not like the other churches were bad or anything. It's just that Jesus seemed to meet me here."

One of the central goals of a discipleship congregation is establishing a context within which individuals and families experience themselves as "connected" to the Divine. There are a number of ways to do this. Vital worship is clearly of central importance. The quality of worship—be it contemporary, traditional, or "blended"—can hinder or aid the accomplishing of this goal. Whatever the style of music, it must be singable with words that make sense to modern people. Sermons must bring the word of God into people's real lives in words they understand, images they can relate to, stories that speak to their experience. Worship leaders must create a sense of divine drama, a sense of sacred space, sacred time, and sacred activity that invites rather than intimidates. The atmosphere of worship must be one of shared expectation: God will be encountered here today. Forgiveness and hope will be experienced here today. Love will be known here today.

It should also be noted, however, that although a discipleship congregation intentionally seeks to create a context within which folks can encounter the Divine, disciples refuse to take on responsibility for the spiritual journeys of others. Disciples do take very seriously our calling to journey with others, and we strive to help them grow deep in the Spirit and the knowledge of the Lord, but we cannot be responsible for whether people choose to grow or learn. That would be the way of codependency and, you will recall, discipleship congregations go the way of interdependency.

In hospice situations, I have watched as loving families stripped away the dignity of their dying loved one. How? Most frequently I observed them ask the dying what they wanted to do for a treatment plan and then overrule them, insisting on a treatment plan that served their pain rather than the dying one's wishes. I learned that people have dignity when they can make decisions *and then live with the consequences of those decisions.*

In the codependent relationships of the membership model, pastors are assumed to be responsible for the spiritual health of the church's members. It is the pastor's fault if he or she cannot keep someone interested in church or the issues of faith. The guilt that most clergy feel when a member hits a spiritual wasteland, officially leaves the church, or simply stops coming can be acute. If we recognize, however, that each of us is ultimately responsible for our own spiritual journey, we will also recognize our responsibility to share in the work of creating a community of faith that provides a positive context for that journey for ourselves and for others. We will share the responsibility of crafting a church that provides opportunities for growth, gives spiritual direction, encourages spiritual discipline, and expects discipleship. Such a community can be shaped without falling into legalism and without usurping the individual's freedom to say either yes or no to God's call "to maturity, to the measure of the full stature of Christ" (Ephesians 4:13).

Finally, the health and vitality of a community of faith are the responsibility of all the faithful and not just their leaders. It is leadership's responsibility to make this clear and to provide vision, direction, and opportunity for growth in discipleship. Whether individuals commit to the vision, follow the direction, and grasp the opportunities for personal growth is up to them.

STAYING THE COURSE

As in all significant changes, successfully moving from a membership model of the church to the discipleship model requires staying the course. The vision of a church that calls each person to committed discipleship with Jesus Christ is compelling. The vision of a church that provides focused worship, teaching, and practical activities that deepen one's experience of God is compelling. The vision of a church that is deliberate in creating a climate of hospitality and mutual compassionate caring is compelling. The vision of a church that is intentional about equipping and encouraging disciples to live their faith wherever they may be and with whomever they may be is compelling. The discipleship model offers a compelling vision, but a daunting one. Many will have a hard time "seeing" it. Many will be frightened and resist it. Many will be attracted but timidly withdraw. Some will grasp the vision and want to move too fast in its direction, leaving others behind. A solid core will emerge with prudent wisdom to shape the vision to the context and stage its implementation. Throughout the move from membership to discipleship, in the face of the many challenges that arise, it will be good to recall over and again that the ending of the journey is in its beginning for those who stay the course. Persistence is the Siamese twin of courage. Perseverance will overcome great barriers and outlast strong opposition.

QUESTIONS FOR PRAYERFUL REFLECTION

1. Is your congregation characterized by centralized pastoral care (only clergy and staff provide the care) or decentralized pastoral care (everybody is trained and encouraged to provide the care)?

2. What do you see as the problems and possibilities of decentralized pastoral care? How would you minimize the problems and maximize the possibilities?

3. Discipleship cultures are gift-based cultures. Are there programs in place in your congregation that encourage the identification and utilization of individuals' gifts? Do people eagerly participate? If not, why not?

4. The culture of a discipleship congregation is hospitable. What programs, activities, and initiatives in your congregation ensure hospitality for strangers in your midst?

5. If your congregation is membership-driven, what steps would need to be taken to change your congregational culture to a discipleship-driven culture? Who needs to be involved? What would be your first steps?

THE ENDING OF THE JOURNEY IS IN
ITS BEGINNING FOR THOSE WHO
STAY THE COURSE.

5
The marks of Discipleship

Can one be Christian without being religious? The vast majority of Americans apparently think so. Polls and opinion surveys indicate that a vast majority of adults in this country think of themselves as Christian. Yet their self-understanding as Christian does not seem to be reflected in their lives in the form of practiced faith. How is this possible?

The story is told about a regional director of a major denomination's global missions department. When visiting China, he was astonished to find on the mainland a thriving, vibrant, growing Christian church of his denomination—without the leadership of missionaries. Missionaries in China had been officially expelled in 1949 with the Communist victory of Mao Tse-tung.

The mission director was also astonished to learn that the Chinese church's adult catechism and membership class was quite intensive, lasting for two years. No one could become a member of that church without going through that process. Upon asking if he, an ordained pastor from their denomination in the United States, could be accepted into their church by simple transfer of membership, they told him: "No. We have worked too hard to earn the trust of the people here. We cannot afford to weaken the community God has given us by letting anyone join without teaching them what our faith means and how it is to be lived."

Faith translates into attitudes and behaviors and thus is far more than simple agreement with a creedal formula.

That church in China grew because its model of the church was a model for discipleship. Its vitality was based upon its conviction that faith translates into attitudes and behaviors and thus is far more than simple agreement with a creedal formula.

What would the Protestant church look like if its members were disciples? To begin with, there would be a positive attempt to translate beliefs into behaviors. The Reformation conviction that good works necessarily follow faith would be reestablished as a foundation stone for church affiliation. The great reformer, Martin Luther, is worth quoting at length here:

> Oh, it is a living, busy, active and mighty thing, this faith. It is impossible for it not to be doing good works incessantly. It does not ask whether good works are to be done, but before the question is asked, it has already done them, and is constantly doing them. Whoever does not do such good works, however, is an unbeliever . . . . Faith is a living, daring confidence in God's grace, so sure and certain

that the believer would stake his life on it a thousand times. This knowledge of and confidence in God's grace makes [people] glad and bold and happy in dealing with God and with all creatures. And this is the work which the Holy Spirit performs in faith. Because of it, without compulsion [Christians are] ready and glad to do good to everyone, to serve everyone, to suffer everything, out of love and praise to God who has shown [them] this grace. Thus it is impossible to separate works from faith, quite as impossible to separate heat and light from fire.[16]

"Faith active in love" is the chief characteristic of a discipleship church, an essential characteristic rooted firmly in the Reformation soil from which the Protestant churches grew.

At Prince of Peace, marks of discipleship have been articulated as some of the practices of faith that will help bridge the gap between beliefs and behaviors. These disciplines of faith are based on biblical and historical practices that have long characterized individuals with living, active faith.

We certainly do not view these practices as a list of spiritual achievements, nor as religious rules. Those who commit to practicing the marks of discipleship are not religious overachievers who are looking to become spiritually superior to others. In fact, the more the marks are practiced, the greater the sense and expression of humility and gratitude to God. This should not surprise us. Historically, those who have, with integrity, sought to integrate their faith into the fabric of their whole lives have shown a greater reluctance to assert themselves and a greater desire to speak of the grace of God at work in and through them.

The marks of discipleship are not institutionally driven. Their origin grew out of our common commitment to do everything possible to equip individuals and families with a real faith for real life. The Protestant principle that all people have ready and equal access to God through Jesus Christ is the foundation stone of this organizational commitment. The goal is to help God's people grow in their spiritual confidence by "practicing the presence of God." A significant assumption is that as we grow in our confidence in God's desire for a real relationship with us and as we more deeply experience the reality of God's presence, we cannot help but connect our faith with our life. Indeed, faith and life become one. When the desire to live all of life from the perspective of faith is built upon God's love and forgiveness for us disclosed in Jesus Christ, the self-imposed expectation of spiritual perfection dims and finally disappears. Disciples don't expect to be perfect. They simply expect to live close to God. They expect to learn, to grow, and to enjoy the abundance of life that Jesus promised. They expect to grow in wisdom as to what God wants for us and from us. This is what the marks of discipleship are all about. Practicing them does not make one perfect. Rather, *practice makes progress.*

THE TRUST FACTOR

As disciples we recognize that all of our strivings are exactly that—strivings in which the desires of our hearts are met with the desires of God's heart. The Holy Spirit gives faith, grows faith, and confirms faith. Our desire is simply to be willing to let God's Spirit work in our lives, whatever that may mean. And here's where trust comes in. To borrow an old truth, disciples trust that "the will of God will not lead you where the grace of God cannot keep you." Such trust opens the disciple to a radical following of the one who calls us to discipleship.

Practicing the marks of discipleship helps us be available and willing before God. They focus our attention on the presence of God and keep our consciousness riveted on God's will for God's world. They open us to the movement of the Spirit and attune our hearing to the still small voice of God. As a fledgling musician who practices her instrument long and hard comes to experience herself as one with the music, so the disciple who practices spiritual disciplines comes to experience herself as one with God. Be it music or spirituality, one enters practice with the trust that the goal will be reached.

LEADERS ARE, ABOVE ALL ELSE, DISCIPLES THEMSELVES

Leaders in the church should not *have* disciples. When they do, the community of faith all too often degenerates into a personality cult. When the leader leaves, the church falls apart. The leader's call is not to gather people around himself or herself, but to gather them around Jesus. The word *disciple* implies a teacher. It is not the leader, but Christ the teacher, at whose feet the disciples—and the leader also—need to sit.

Leaders of Christ's church must be people who consciously affirm their own desire to live and grow as disciples of Christ. Church leadership, be it ordained or not ordained, is not, properly speaking, a profession. It is a calling. Leaders are called to follow Christ in such a way that they encourage and enable others to enter into the same discipleship into which they have entered.

Leaders increasingly must recognize that the "business" of the church is not business but the fulfillment of the church's mission. The best practices of business and nonprofits must be put to use, not as ends in themselves, but as servants to the higher calling of discipleship. Evangelism and stewardship, women's and men' ministries, youth ministry, Sunday school, worship, social justice ministries, and even pastoral care must be held accountable to this one question: how does what we are doing encourage and enable others to live lives of active faith? Whatever programs and practices, activities and events cannot be justified as directly contributing to this goal must be reevaluated, reshaped, or let go. The church serves God by "making disciples" of God's people and teaching them to observe all that Christ has commanded us. Leaders of the church must commit to this principle—and live it.

Faith Does Make a Difference

When a congregation commits to practicing the marks of discipleship, it has, as it were, raised the bar. It is simply assumed that faith will make a difference in how we live.

When I was riding with a member of the church not long ago, I noticed that on his rearview mirror he had a green dot. At Prince of Peace, we use green dots as a visual reminder to pray. I asked him why he had a dot there, and he replied, "When I see that dot, it reminds me to pray. And I drive less aggressively, more graciously."

I wondered how many other members and friends of Prince of Peace have a green dot on their rearview mirrors. And then I wondered what would happen if more and more people had a visual reminder of their faith while they drove. How would that impact the phenomenon of road rage?

The Power of Expectation

The discipleship model expects the Christian community—through Word and Sacrament—to transform lives. It is a sad commentary on our worship life in the church that so many of our leaders and worshipers have given up—if they ever had it—the hope that our spiritual practices will actually change lives. When we expect change as a result of encountering

God in worship, in music, prayer, reading, the spoken word, bread and wine and water, change happens. When we expect change through Christian teaching, Bible study, and holy conversation, change happens.

The power of expectation spreads through a congregation when the conviction that God does indeed transform lives through God's boundless grace is believed, expressed, and experienced by the church's leaders. When the life of the church is formed by this conviction, the power of expectation reaches throughout the community and touches everyone from the child in her parent's arms to the elderly in nursing. Change happens. Lives are transformed.

My friend with the green dot on his rearview mirror was no longer content to simply react to traffic out of old patterns of impatience, anger, and resentment. He wanted to change his attitudes and behaviors in driving to become, as it were, more Christlike. He wanted patience, gentleness, generosity, self-control—the "fruits of the Spirit"—to characterize his driving. The simple act of putting a green dot on his rearview mirror reminded him of who he was and whose he was. It turned him to prayer—repentance for his poor driving when needed, intercession for other drivers when needed, thanksgiving for changing attitudes and behaviors when they were experienced. The little green dot focused his attention on the immediate presence of God and opened him to new ways of responding in love to situations that previously only irritated and annoyed him. Whenever such things happen, faith and life are experienced as one. When that happens, our behavior begins to encourage positive change in others as we shape our responses to them from our faith in the God who calls us to participate in God's love for the world.

The message of the Scriptures is the message of God's continual turning to the world in love. This God does not call Christians to simply react to the world but to proactively engage the world, to stand against the violence, the greed, the enmity, the self-centeredness, the fear, against everything that destroys life, that turns God's good creation into a wasteland. The marks of discipleship are wellsprings from which people of faith drink deeply of the Spirit and gain the wisdom, courage, and strength to be the world's greatest lovers.

AN INVITATION TO SERIOUS FAITH

At Prince of Peace, members, friends, and visitors are given a credit card–sized white plastic card to either stick in their wallets, put on their refrigerators, carry in their pockets, or perhaps use as a bookmark. On the front of the card we have printed in bold letters the words *Marks of Discipleship* along with the words *Power Surge*. With these few words, we communicate our conviction that it is the committed discipleship of God's people that releases the power of the Holy Spirit in the ministries and mission of the church.

On the reverse side of the card we list what we have found to be the basic or foundational practices of those who seek to live active lives of faith as disciples of Christ.

> **To the glory of God, I believe I am called...**
> *"to the measure of the full stature of Christ." –Eph. 4:12*
>
> **I will strive to...**
> • **PRAY** daily
> • **WORSHIP** weekly
> • **READ** the Bible
> • **SERVE** at and beyond Prince of Peace
> • Be in **RELATIONSHIP** to encourage spiritual growth in others
> • **GIVE** of my time, talents and resources

Clearly, the six marks of discipleship that we list and seek commitment to at Prince of Peace are not an exhaustive list of all the spiritual disciplines that a Christian might practice. In our experience, however, they are foundational practices that, over time, become the bedrock upon which lives of faithful discipleship are built. The are the sine qua non, or essential practices, of a community of faith that is moving from membership to discipleship.

On the surface they may seem overly simple and obvious to the point that they seem to go without saying. Don't be mistaken. They are simple and yet profound. And obvious though they may be, far more lip service than seriousness is paid to them in most congregations.

In Zen Buddhism, even experienced practitioners are admonished to maintain a beginner's mind. The beginner's humility, openness, simplicity, and eagerness to learn should not be lost with time and experience. This is good advice for Christians, as well. These simple foundational practices, woven into the fabric of daily life, can never be outgrown and will always be sources of continued growth, strength, understanding, wisdom, and insight, as well as joy and delight in God's presence—but only for those who have a beginner's mind. Those who either think they have "arrived" at spiritual maturity or are jaded to the point of skepticism will either spurn or belittle these simple practices as being of no value. Those with a beginner's capacity for wonder, however, will simply do them expectantly and so enter into the mystery of God.

THE FIRST MARK OF A DISCIPLE: DAILY PRAYER

Frankly, I was stunned. He approached me after worship and said, "I have really enjoyed the sermon series you and the other pastors have given on prayer. And I really feel called to pray more. The only problem I have is that I just don't know how."

When Rod Kopp, our director of finance and personnel at Prince of Peace, offered a workshop at our annual Changing Church Conference on prayer, we were all excited by the number of participants who attended. But I was stunned again when one of the pastors responded to Rod's workshop with a startling confession. "You are assuming," he said, "that we pastors know how to pray. But many of us don't."

This problem of not knowing how to pray is not a new one. Some two thousand years ago, Jesus "was praying in a certain place, and after he had finished, one of his disciples said to him, 'Lord teach us to pray'" (Luke 11:1). Prayer can be taught—and learned.

A discipleship church recognizes the need to teach people how to pray. This is not difficult. We have all learned how to talk to each other. We know how to share our needs with people who care about us and can help us, how to give and receive information, how to ask for things, how to express gratitude, how to say we are sorry and ask for forgiveness, how to say what's important to us and, perhaps most important, how to speak words of love and delight to those in whom we love and delight. And we know how to listen to others when

> A discipleship church recognizes the need to teach people how to pray.

they speak in similar ways to us. Prayer is simply doing what we already know how to do, but with God as the one to whom we speak and to whom we listen.

The real difficulty is not in learning how to say what's on our hearts and minds (although most of us could stand to brush up on both our self-knowledge and our communication skills). The real difficulty is in creating a context in which conversation with God is as natural and expected as conversation among families, friends, and acquaintances.

It begins with the leadership. Remember the story about the staff person who expressed both surprise and delight when I told her that in our emerging discipleship church, time spent in personal prayer in her office was as valued a part of her job as time spent in meetings, teaching, counseling, or writing reports? When prayer is as natural as breathing to those who lead, it soon becomes as natural as breathing to those who follow. When prayer is a wellspring from which the leader obviously drinks living water, all those around him or her begin to thirst for some of the same. The words of the psalmist will become the song of your congregation:

O God, you are my God, I seek you,
   my soul thirsts for you;
my flesh faints for you,
   as in a dry and weary land where there is no water.
So I have looked upon you in the sanctuary,
   beholding your power and glory.
Because your steadfast love is better than life,
   my lips will praise you.
So I will bless you as long as I live;
   I will lift up my hands and call on your name.
My soul is satisfied as with a rich feast,
   and my mouth praises you with joyful lips
when I think of you on my bed,
   and meditate on you in the watches of the night;
for you have been my help
   and in the shadow of your wings I sing for joy.
(Psalm 63:1-7)

Leaders—through their own prayerful attitudes and behavior—create a space for people where expressing the desire of your heart and the thirsting of your soul is not only safe but encouraged. Sociologists would call it a plausibility structure—a community that encourages, supports, and reinforces ways of thinking, feeling, and behaving that express the core beliefs and values of the group.

As I mentioned earlier, at Prince of Peace we reconsidered using the printed prayers of our worship book and opted for replacing them with spontaneous prayer as a way of modeling prayer for the congregation. It gave all of us a new sense of freedom and authenticity in prayer that carries over into all the activities of the congregation, activities that are always punctuated with appropriate prayer at appropriate times.

We have learned much—and continue to learn—about the rhythms of discursive prayer, prayer that uses words to express our petitions and intercessions, our laments and suffering, our fears and hopes, our thanksgiving and joy, our love and praise. But prayer can go far beyond words, we've learned, as we've become more familiar with the rhythms of nondiscursive prayer, prayers of silence and simple presence to the divine. It wasn't long after the small group of women introduced the staff to centering prayer, for instance, that we recognized the value of that prayer of silence for the whole community and incorporated it into public worship.

We took Psalm 46 seriously: "Be still and know that I am God" (10). "For God alone my soul waits in silence," writes the psalmist (62:5). And the prophet writes, "The Lord is in his holy temple; let all the earth keep silence before him!" (Habakkuk 2:20). And we began to create moments of silence before God in our Sunday worship.

We began to take time in worship to talk about—and to practice—centering prayer. Instruction was given and worshipers were invited to enter the silence and simply be in the loving presence of God, letting the silence communicate the love in their own hearts for God. Often the preacher of the day would conclude the sermon with an invitation to be still before God in loving silence. The sense of God's presence in the stillness of the sanctuary and the stillness of our hearts is dramatic.

Of course, prayer is never coercive. No one is forced to practice centering prayer either in or outside of worship, although all are encouraged to do so. Silence is difficult, if not frightening, for people in our noisy, high-speed, always-doing-something world. Silence is an acquired taste, and it takes some time for frantic and frenetic people to become comfortable with it.

Although contemplative or meditative forms of prayer, such as centering prayer, have a long history in Christian tradition, they are not very familiar to modern Protestants. Thus it takes instruction and example and time to create a climate where the silence of centering prayer is as natural and desirable as the words of our conversational prayer.

If you desire to integrate moments of silence and centering prayer into public worship, be clear about what is going on and then invite people to just sit and let the moment pass if they are uncomfortable or unsure and don't want to prayerfully enter the silence. When presented as an opportunity to experience something new and positive, most people will give it a try. With patience a congregation can be brought to value silence and to experience within it the loving presence of God.

> The church's responsibility is simply to provide opportunities to learn and experience the many ways and wonders of prayer.

Discipleship churches are schools of prayer. The church's responsibility is not to control whether or how anyone prays, but simply to provide opportunities to learn and experience the many ways and wonders of prayer.

THE SECOND MARK OF A DISCIPLE: WEEKLY WORSHIP

From the very beginning of the church, in the days after Jesus' resurrection and ascension, the life of the community of faith has revolved around the regular gathering of believers for worship, common prayer, and eating bread and drinking wine in remembrance of the one in whose name they gathered. Worship is the linchpin of a discipleship church. It is in the gathering of God's people around Word and Sacrament that the community of faith affirms its calling, receives the gifts of grace, is nourished and strengthened, and sent back into the world to love as God loves. To absent oneself from worship is akin to a hungry person turning away from a free meal. (Of course, the quality of the cooking might be enough to make a hungry person do exactly that!)

Although not impossible, it is nonetheless true that public worship will rarely rise above the spirits of those who lead in worship. No stately liturgy, hallowed and ancient hymns, anthems with organ and choir can make up for clergy and worship assistants who simply go through the motions, handling tradition by rote. And no amount of high-tech accoutrements, loud and lively contemporary music, bands and praise groups can make up for clergy and worship assistants who see themselves as "on stage" before the congregation rather than before God.

Those who lead in worship must worship—not just do a job. If they are open to and aware of the wonder, the awesomeness, and the mystery of God truly present in Word and Sacrament, in proclamation and praise, and in music and singing, and if their manner in presiding reflects their own feelings of awe in God's presence, the congregation will be drawn into the sacred drama where God sits enthroned on the praises of God's people (Psalm 22:3). For good or for ill, leadership in worship is rooted in the dynamics of a leader's life of faith.

For the leaders of worship—and the gathered worshipers— the hour on Sunday morning or Saturday evening or any other time is a step into the presence of the living God they serve throughout the week. Worship is both the culmination of discipleship and the matrix from which discipleship is formed. Disciples worship not out of obligation, but out of eagerness. The presence of God mediated through the grace of worship is a "foretaste of the feast to come," food for the journey.

It is important, of course, to pay careful attention to the form and structure of worship, the language of music and preaching, and the balance between solemnity and celebration.

Worship planning should focus on two central questions: What can we do to facilitate an encounter between God and God's people? What can we do to ensure that worship is genuinely participatory and not merely a spectator sport? Keep in mind when answering those questions, however, that, as said before, no amount of tinkering with the outward elements of worship can take the place of worship leaders who are caught up in the wonder and mystery of God. To deepen the quality of worship for disciples and seekers alike, those who lead in worship must be folks who tend to their own discipleship.

Disciples worship. Their very lives are expressions of trust and praise to the God who made them, loves them, and invites them to love as God loves. Everything that happens in a discipleship church moves to and from that holy moment when God's people gather together in worship.

The Third Mark of a Disciple: Bible Reading

- 91 percent of all households in the United States own at least one Bible.
- The typical household owns three Bibles.
- 38 percent of adults in the U.S. read the Bible during a typical week—not including when they are at church.
- Among Bible readers, the average amount of time spent reading the Bible during an entire week is fifty-two minutes—or, about ten minutes a day.[17]

The book is out there, but apparently it gathers more dust than readers. Again we are faced with the fact that making a paradigm shift from a membership model to a discipleship model requires crafting a new congregational culture. In the membership model, the Bible is a tool for the pastor and, at best, an accessory for the average member. In the discipleship model, the Bible is a part of everyone's tool kit.

If most of us opened a carpenter's tool kit, we wouldn't know what to do with most of what we found inside. Using the tools of any trade requires the development of skills through mentoring, practice, and experience. It's no different with the Bible, the key tool in the discipleship trade.

"Pastor," he said, "I really understand the need to read the Bible daily. In fact, when I don't do it, my world kind of gets out of whack. My problem is that I don't know how to get past some of what I read. I mean, not only do I not understand it, I don't even like it!"

Comments like these are neither uncommon nor surprising. We will continue to hear them until our churches become communities where folks are not only expected to read the Bible, but are equipped to do it. The expectation is important and needs to be clearly communicated, but without providing people with nonintimidating, practical opportunities for learning how to use this tool it will all come to naught, and the tool will stay in the tool kit—unused.

The reality that the Bible is at the center of our life together, and this foundation of our individual lives of discipleship needs to be continually made evident. At Prince of Peace, for example, we have placed Bibles between our chairs in the worship center—and we use them. Whenever possible and appropriate, we ask our worshipers to open the Bible, either to follow along or read to aloud with the reader. We don't assume that people know where to find things, so we give clues—"the Gospel of Mark is the second book in the New Testament"—and then we give page numbers so the worshipers can find the text without embarrassment or confusion. The point is simply to get people used to opening the Bible, to get them familiar with its contents and language, and to get them thinking about—and experiencing—the ways in which it can be used to support the life of faith. We also let everyone who comes to worship know that the Bibles between the chairs are also there for anyone who needs one to take home and keep—no questions asked.

It is important to provide ongoing learning opportunities in both the personal and corporate use of Scripture. Classes in how to read, study, and pray with the Bible should regularly be offered and opportunities to develop skills with the other tools of the trade—commentaries, concordances, Bible dictionaries, and atlases—should be provided as well. Beginning, intermediate, and advanced classes, both in study methods and in biblical content and application, should be made available and widely promoted. Small-group Bible studies, readily available print and electronic resources in the church library, a time for biblical reflection on the agenda of every meeting, articles on the meaning and application of biblical texts in the church newsletter, Bible memory challenges for kids and adults alike—there is no end to the things you can do to create an environment in which turning to the Bible is as natural as reading the daily newspaper.

> It is important to provide ongoing learning opportunities in both the personal and corporate use of Scripture.

Again, let me stress the importance of leadership. As critical as it is to provide people with opportunities and encouragement to become comfortable with using the Bible as a tool in their discipleship, the chance that they will avail themselves of those opportunities goes way up when they experience their leaders as individuals who live in and out of the Word of God. Christian leaders must know the Bible. No one would want a heart surgeon who has not learned, and continues to refine his use of, the tools of the trade. No one should have a Christian leader who does not do the same.

THE FOURTH MARK OF A DISCIPLE: SERVICE

Remember the words of the prophet Micah and his one-line definition of the spiritual life: "What does the Lord require of you but to do justice, and to love kindness, and to walk humbly with your God?" There is no getting around it. The life of a disciple involves service. The Gospel of John tells us that "God so loved the world that he gave his only son" (John 3:16) and that God intends to keep on loving the world through us, God's beloved disciples of Jesus (John 13:34-35). Justice and love are not options for those who follow Jesus. Service is a key mark of discipleship.

It is often assumed, falsely, that service directly involves the church. It may, but it need not. Much of the service that Christians carry out for the sake of the world God loves happens far from any direct connection with the church. Effective church leaders need to know, as much as possible, what their people are doing in the world and to what arenas of service their faith in Christ and calling to discipleship have brought them. Disciples' contributions to the well-being of God's world and those who live in it need to be recognized, acknowledged, and celebrated. Their stories need to be told. Again, it is a matter of creating a culture that affirms discipleship and its extension to all of life, not just life in the church.

The programs of a discipleship church will provide people with both a menu of opportunities to serve and the encouragement to serve. There is no end of need, and a discipleship church will provide a variety of opportunities to engage people at their points of greatest passion, interest, skill, and ability. The marks of discipleship already discussed—prayer, worship, and Bible study—all lead to this end: participation in God's love for the world and service that leads to greater well-being for all, particularly for those in greatest need or at greatest risk.

Whether a disciple serves directly in the programs of the church or serves through other agencies finally makes no difference. The community of faith is wonderfully present whenever and wherever its people "give a cup of cold water" in the name of Jesus.

Any discussion of service will inevitably raise the issue of boundaries. How do disciples give their service to the church and the community and not get lost in a black hole of never-ending duty? How do disciples avoid burnout? Ironically, the church seems to be filled with a lot of folks who are underused, some folks who are overused, and hardly any who have achieved a healthy balance in the area of service. Four things can be said:

1. A church that has created a lively atmosphere where service is expected, acknowledged, valued, and celebrated is likely to attract more people into service, thus spreading the work around and providing opportunities for breathing space for everyone.

2. A church that is intentional about providing training opportunities that give people skills and confidence in various kinds of service is also likely to attract more people into service. People are more likely to serve when they are confident that they will be trained to the point that they can do well what they are asked to do.

3. A church that continually reminds its disciples that service begins at home and in the workplace, as we strive to build healthy relationships, seek reconciliation, resolve conflicts, and simply care for the people closest to us is also more likely to attract more people into structured programs of service. People whose discipleship is lived out in compassionate caring, generosity, and helpfulness to those closest to them are more likely to see the needs of those further away and want to do something about them.

4. A church that sees the well-being of all people as the desire of God will respect its disciples' right to say "No" when

asked to serve and will encourage those who are obviously overextended to step back for a while and let others carry the load.

The culture of a membership church assumes that the church, its staff, and the "few who do everything" are there to serve the membership. The culture of a discipleship church is strikingly different for those who know that they are followers of the "Son of Man who came not to be served, but to serve" (Matthew 20:28).

The Fifth Mark of a Disciple: Spiritual Friendships

We met in my office. I was meeting with all of the staff, one-on-one, about the marks of discipleship. This meeting was with my administrative assistant, Mary Jeanne.

"I'd like to talk with you," I began, "about the marks of discipleship. As you know, we have taken the position as a church that all of our leaders must commit to support and practice these foundational spiritual disciplines. This is not about becoming a super Christian, Mary Jeanne. This is about growing spiritually strong and confident in God's love."

We then walked through each of the marks. We talked freely about them, and she candidly shared with me where she was felt she strong and where she thought she would have to work a little harder. By the time we were done talking, there was no doubt about her commitment to the marks or her willingness to grow in her own practice of them.

Later, when someone raised questions about whether the marks of discipleship were legalistic or not, I asked Mary Jeanne how she felt about the process we had been through, the expectations of the staff, and the practice of the marks. She didn't hesitate for a moment in expressing her genuine enthusiasm.

"I thought it was great," she replied. "No one has ever cared about my spiritual life before."

Though her comment was perhaps overstated, I believe that the Protestant church has failed to create an environment in which spiritual growth is both expected and nurtured. Where growth is not expected, it rarely happens. Where it is not nourished, it is stunted. At Prince of Peace, we expect people to grow spiritually and we believe that such growth is best nurtured through spiritual friendships and mutual accountability around our common commitment to the marks of discipleship.

No one, not even the senior pastor, is above being held accountable for his or her spiritual health and growth. We demonstrate real care for each other when we ask how things are going in our practice of the marks of discipleship—not as a way of keeping tabs on one another, but as a method of genuine support and encouragement. We learn from each other's experience. We walk with each other through the inevitable dry places and "dark nights of the soul."

We encourage individuals to form spiritual friendships and to agree to hold each other accountable for conscientious practice of the marks. Spiritual friends pray for and with each other, encourage each other, share insights into Scripture, and help one another reflect on the ways God is present and active in their lives. Our cultural expectation of spiritual growth is clearly expressed in the common worship goal at Prince of Peace: "The bull's-eye for our ministry is to equip you with a real faith for your real life by the power of the Gospel and the presence of the Holy Spirit."

> It is in interpersonal, caring relationships between committed disciples that real growth takes place.

It is critically important to our staff that the worshiping congregation know of our deep commitment to assist them in growing in God's grace "to the measure of the full stature of Christ." We are about the business of spiritual formation and have discovered that it is in interpersonal, caring relationships between committed disciples that real growth takes place. Disciples covet such spiritual friendships and relish in the accountability they bring to the practice of discipleship.

THE SIXTH MARK OF A DISCIPLE: GIVING

In the *Lutheran Book of Worship*, the prayer of the congregation following the giving of the weekly offering reads:

> Merciful Father, we offer with joy and thanksgiving what you have first given us—our selves, our time, and our possessions, signs of your gracious love. Receive them for the sake of him who offered himself for us, Jesus Christ our Lord. Amen.

The words of this prayer sound different when prayed in a discipleship church. In a membership-driven church, the offering is analogous to the payment of dues, a fee for services received. In a discipleship church, the offering is symbolic of the giving of one's self to the God who loves us with an everlasting love. It is not done begrudgingly, but with "joy and thanksgiving." For disciples, giving should be as natural as receiving.

That may seem a "hard saying" in a self-centered, acquisitive world where cultural convention determines a person's worth by how much they have, not by how much they give away. But the hardness softens when the heart softens in wonder and gratitude for the immensity of God's many and varied gifts to us.

Once again we are faced with the need to challenge and change the culture of the church. A membership-driven culture is characterized by an entitlement mentality. A discipleship-driven culture is characterized by a generosity rooted in the generosity of God. A membership church asks for money (and people resent it). A discipleship church simply reminds people in many and varied ways that life is pure gift and that the giver of life is liberal in sustaining life with every good and beautiful thing (and people give). It is called "consciousness raising"—creating opportunities for people to consider what's real and respond in faith.

At Prince of Peace, we have, as it were, put our money where our mouth is. We no longer ask for annual pledges. We have come to believe that the Holy Spirit will guide the giving of those who have heard of God's generosity and are open to the teaching of God's Word. So we encourage people to prepare a giving plan—one that only they and God know about. When the plan is completed, we ask them to seal it in a self-addressed, stamped envelope. On a given Sunday, the people process to the altar and leave their giving plans there, in sealed envelopes, before God and the congregation. In a few weeks, we send them back, unopened, to our worshipers. We have no idea what will be given in the coming year. The first year's results were startling—a 13 percent increase in overall giving!

At Prince of Peace, we teach tithing as a reasonable, biblically based model for giving. This is not a legalism with us but a discipline for disciples and thus a matter of individual conscience. We want disciples to understand that tithing is much more than a matter of obedience. Setting aside 10 percent of take-home pay as a gift in support of ministry and mission is a discipline that keeps us focused on a number of spiritual truths.

First, we are continually reminded of who the giver of all our abundance really is. God is the creator of all we are and have. Practicing the tithe reminds us of our total dependence upon God. It keeps us focused on generosity and makes us cogivers with God as our gifts are used by the body of Christ to bring blessing to others.

Second, tithing has the capacity to put the things of this world into perspective. There is nothing inherently wrong with wealth or possessions. As the writer of 1 Timothy reminds us, it is not money, but "the love of money" that is "a root of all kinds of evil" (6:10). Jesus reminds us that no one can serve God and wealth (Matthew 6:24). Disciples by definition serve God. Tithing is an ongoing reminder of where our loyalties belong. It keeps us focused with our attention fixed on what is finally important. And it gives clarity to Jesus' teaching: "Do not store up for yourselves treasures on earth, where moth and rust consume and where thieves break in and steal; but store up for yourselves treasures in heaven, where neither moth nor rust consume and where thieves do not break in and steal. For where your treasure is, there will your heart be also" (Matthew 6:19-21). The disciple's heart belongs with God. Tithing as a spiritual discipline helps keep it there.

Third, like all spiritual disciplines, tithing often leads people beyond their original expectations. Many, if not most, of the people I have known who began to tithe didn't stop there. They began with a commitment to grow to a full tithe, but once that goal was reached, they continued to expand their giving. They did so not out of duty, but out of joy and a deep abiding trust in the goodness of God. Those who come to understand the meaning of tithing also come to understand that the "offering" begins after the tithe is given. This is a true transformation of the heart—the goal of spiritual disciplines.

I will never forget a conversation I had with a friend who was seeking contributions to the church. He told me that he had just received a check made out in six figures. I was amazed and expected him to continue and tell me how pleased he was with his performance in securing this significant gift. Knowing him, I should have known better. Instead of boasting, he grinned and said, "And that's my next goal, too. I can't wait until I can write a check like that!" The delight in his eyes was infectious and that's reason enough to teach tithing.

"For if the eagerness is there, the gift is acceptable according to what one has— not according to what one does not have" (2 Corinthians 8:12). Providing disciples with the tools to make an honest assessment of their financial realities and then helping them to consider what steps they might make to move toward a tithe is a leadership responsibility. It is a responsibility, however, that can only be met credibly by leaders who tithe themselves.

Living in Grace

The marks of discipleship have nothing to do with a legalistic, law-oriented approach to Christian faith. The purpose is not to create super Christians or any kind of spiritual elite. No one earns salvation or gains any special favor from God by practicing the marks. They are simply habits of the soul that open us to the wonder and mystery of God's active presence in our lives. They keep us focused; they fix our attention on the things of God.

When the marks of discipleship are adopted and practiced by an individual, growth happens. When adopted and practiced by a group of individuals, greater growth happens, because of the mutual encouragement, reinforcement, and support that come from common commitment. When adopted by a whole congregation, not everybody will get on board. Some will be skeptical, uninterested, or intimidated. Some may leave the congregation, while others may stay without participating. But when adopted by a whole congregation and practiced by many, a climate of change is introduced, an atmosphere of excitement and expectation prevails, thus creating a context that encourages the timid or resistant to give it a try.

When we give our white plastic card with the marks of discipleship printed on it to all who worship at Prince of Peace, we are, in effect, saying, "This is who we are; this is what we do." No apologies, no embarrassment, and no boasting. It's just who we are, for in the grace of God we have chosen discipleship.

As important as the practice of the marks of discipleship are to every Christian, it is remarkable to see their effect on leaders in the church. Most pastors and lay professional staff entered the ministry of the church because of deeply felt experiences of the forgiving, redeeming presence of God in their lives. The call to ministry is experienced as grace; the response to the call is experienced as grace. Most workers in the church begin with the strong desire to "render service with enthusiasm, as to the Lord" (Ephesians 6:7), and their ministry is motivated by the experience of a lived relationship with Christ.

But, in a membership-driven church, it is often not long before the demands of a chaplaincy ministry shift the focus from mission to the member and from God to the "business" of the church. The result—either clergy and staff burn out or become small, ineffectual, and turned in on themselves. The need to continually and personally care for the members, provide the services they seek, always be on call, and keep the "business" of the church going by resolving conflict and keeping everyone happy to keep the offering flowing—all this and more drain the energy and distract the souls of clergy and staff from the one thing necessary (Luke 10:41-42). "Worried and distracted by many things," all too many clergy and staff fail to tend to their own spirituality and end up losing the joy of their salvation. The irony is that if pastors and staff would spend sufficient time looking to their own spiritual growth and teaching others how to do the same, rather than exhausting themselves in an impossible chaplaincy ministry to the whole membership, everyone's needs would be taken care of. The community of disciples would see to it.

For Christian leaders, the marks of discipleship are an invitation back to the reason they entered the ministry of the church. The marks are a call to commit again to practicing the faith that once claimed us, transformed us, and set us free: "He has told you, O mortal, what is good; and what does the Lord require of you but to do justice, to love kindness, and to walk humbly with your God?" (Micah 6:8).

> For Christian leaders, the marks of discipleship are an invitation back to the reason they entered the ministry of the church.

And that, finally, is what the marks of discipleship are all about—equipping Christians to do what the Lord requires. It is the long experience of the Christian church that walking humbly with our God—which practicing the marks of discipleship assists—is the surest way to justice and kindness.

Psalm 51 contains a prayer that can speak to the hearts of Christian leaders who have lost the vitality and enthusiasm for ministry and mission that first characterized their work and who feel distanced from the God who called them to this work:

Create in me a clean heart, O God,
    and put a new and right spirit within me.
Do not cast me away from your presence,
    and do not take your holy spirit from me.
Restore to me the joy of your salvation,
    and sustain in me a willing spirit.

The practice of the marks of discipleship is a channel of grace through which God can answer this simple and yet profound prayer. God's grace meets the desire of the heart through the disciplines that express that desire.

QUESTIONS FOR PRAYERFUL REFLECTION

1. Which of the marks of discipleship are strengths for you and which are areas where growth is needed?

	Strength	Growth
Daily prayer		
Weekly worship		
Bible reading		
Service in and beyond the church		
Spiritual friendships		
Giving time, talents, and resources		

What might you do to turn areas of growth into areas of strength?

2. Is the leadership of your congregation committed to the personal practice of spiritual disciplines? Does it seem important that they have such a commitment? Why or why not?

3. Are regular worshipers encouraged to commit to the personal practice of spiritual disciplines? Does it seem important that they have such a commitment? Why or why not?

4. How can both the leadership and those who worship in your congregation be mentored in effective spiritual practices?

5. What are the possibilities and dangers of spiritual friendships? How can you capitalize on the possibilities and guard against the dangers?

GOD'S GRACE MEETS THE DESIRE
OF THE HEART THROUGH THE
DISCIPLINES THAT EXPRESS
THAT DESIRE.

6

Beliefs, values, vision, and mission

"**I** am really glad to be with you today," I said. "Most of you know me, but I don't know you . . . or much about you."

It was my first chance to meet with this particular group of new members. It was a large group, as we were receiving more than ninety-five families. Now, as I stood before them, I hoped to connect with them in a meaningful way.

"I wonder," I asked, "how many of you worshiped with us for more than a year before you decided to join?" Nearly all the hands in the room went up.

"How many have been worshiping for more than two years? Three?" Most of the hands stayed up.

By this time I was very curious. "How many of you wor-shiped with us for more than five years before making the decision to join?" I was astonished to discover that more than half of the adults in the room had been worshiping for more than five years before deciding to become members of our congregation.

Later, during the question-and-answer time, I learned that many of them waited that long simply because they wanted to know what we believed and how serious we were about our beliefs. They wanted time to listen, observe, ques-tion, and experience what Prince of Peace was all about. Having come to know what we believe and having experi-enced our struggles to be consistent with what we say we believe, they were now ready to commit to our ministry and mission by officially joining the church. For serious Chris-tians, this is not uncommon and should be interpreted as a positive challenge to a congregation to know itself and to live the faith it confesses.

BEING CLEAR ABOUT BELIEFS AND VALUES

There was a time when questions about the beliefs and val-ues of any given congregation could easily be answered by reference to the church's denominational affiliation. Identify a church as Presbyterian and you knew that the notion of God's sovereignty was of central importance. Identify a church as Lutheran and you knew that the "ministry of Word and Sacrament" would be in the center of things. Enter a Baptist church and you knew you'd find a theology of free will expressed in baptism as a declaration of faith. Denomi-nations were essentially clusters of congregations and min-istries with a common theology, common forms of worship, a common polity, and a common view of the world. Move from church to church within any denomination and you could expect to experience the familiarity of family.

And people pretty much did exactly that. A change of address might lead to a change of church but not a change of denomination. Lutherans looked for a new Lutheran church. Baptists, Presbyterians, Methodists, Episcopalians, Congregationalists—whatever you were, that's the kind of church you looked for when settling in a new place. Denominational loyalty was high, as was denominational homogeneity. Not so anymore.

Denominations are becoming wildly heterogeneous. Theological diversity, liturgical diversity, and diversity in polity and governance are becoming the order of the day. Churches in all denominations are increasingly shaping themselves in unique ways in response to their own peculiar contexts and "one size fits all" is no longer the case.

No wonder visitors to our churches are taking much longer to decide whether to join. Like those in our New Disciples Class at Prince of Peace, they want to know what the community of faith where they have come to worship really believes and practices. They know that the denominational label is no longer a clear indicator of what they will find inside, and they will take as much time as they need to figure it out.

We can bemoan the twin loss of denominational homogeneity and denominational loyalty, or we can see it as a fresh blowing of the wind of the Spirit and trust that the God who established and loves the church will not abandon it but rather will lead it into new times.

Spelling Out Your Beliefs

As a result of this denominational confusion, churches that are interested in attracting new worshipers are discovering the need to be out front and clear about who they are, what they believe, and how they practically go about being the body of Christ in the world. Increasingly, congregations that are moving to the discipleship model are spelling out their biblical and theological positions.

Such statements of belief are foundational. They define the local congregation. From stating their position on the Bible and the historic creeds of the church to their position on issues emerging from our contemporary cultural context, discipleship congregations are finding the need to make clear where they stand.

At Prince of Peace we have two statements of beliefs. The first is in our official constitution, which states:

> This congregation accepts all the canonical books of the Old and New Testaments as the inspired and revealed Word of God . . . and accepts and confesses the ancient ecumenical creeds: the Apostolic, the Nicene and the Athanasian; and the Unaltered Augsburg Confession and Luther's Small Catechism. Also the documents in the Book of Concord of 1580. . . .

This is an important statement and, to the theologically and historically learned, quite meaningful, but it begs the question: "What does that mean in real life?"

To answer this legitimate question, we have written a statement of the beliefs that shape Prince of Peace. The statement is published and made available to any who are interested. It reads:

The Foundation of Prince of Peace

Prince of Peace teaches that our God:
1. Has created and is sustaining all that exists and his truth is revealed to us in the Holy Bible;
2. Has entered human history in the crucified and

risen Savior, Jesus of Nazareth, that we might know we are loved and empowered by God's grace alone;

3. Works through the church for the redemption of creation by the power of the Holy Spirit;

4. Changes lives through the gospel of Jesus Christ, calling Christians to lives of:

   a. Continuing renewal

   b. Discovery of new ways to communicate and live out the gospel of Jesus Christ before the world

   c. Welcome and witness to all no matter where they are on life's journey of faith

   d. Practicing compassion and justice as signs of Christ's presence in the world;

5. Has provided a foundation for ministry in the historical witness of the Christian church especially in the ecumenical creeds and the Lutheran Confession.

This is the position statement of Prince of Peace, which translates our confessional stance into language ordinary people can understand. Whatever the denominational affiliation, or lack of one, a congregation defines itself as a particular ministry when it makes a statement of beliefs that is understandable and accessible to anyone. This doesn't mean that further clarification isn't

> A congregation defines itself as a particular ministry when it makes a statement of beliefs that is understandable and accessible to anyone.

necessary, but the basic position of the congregation can be easily grasped.

The visitor or first-time worshiper can, at a glance, understand where the congregation stands, where its focus is, how it lives our common faith. Thus visitors can understand up front whether the church fits with their own understanding and spirituality. To accomplish this goal, the statement of beliefs cannot be written in unfamiliar theological language, and it ought to be short, clear, and to the point.

Spelling out a faith community's foundational beliefs in clear accessible language is based on a number of assumptions. First, it assumes that people have the right to know what we believe as soon as they have an interest in our community. Second, it assumes that not every worshiper will find a spiritual home in any one congregation. This leads to the liberating notion that congregations in the same area need not be in competition with one another but can actually serve the faith—and God's people—in a complementary fashion.

From Prince of Peace's statement of beliefs, it should be clear that, over time, those who wear the traditional labels of either left-wing liberal Christians or right-wing conservative Christians would probably be uncomfortable at Prince of Peace. We are, in the stereotypical sense, neither liberal nor conservative. We are "conservative" in the sense that we are quite interested in conserving historic Christian values, beliefs, and practices that have stood the test of time, but we are neither fundamentalist nor are we afraid of change. And we are "liberal" in the sense that we believe God's grace is a fountain of liberality. God's mercy and justice, forgiveness and redemption are generously available to all and we are committed to act as an agent of God's liberality in the midst of our postmodern world.

A congregation's statement of beliefs is a public acknowledgment of its theological, biblical, and practical focus. St. Paul may have been able to be "all things to all people" but our churches cannot. Biblical and theological integrity demands that we make our positions clear. Those for whom they are not satisfactory will most likely be better served—and better serve—elsewhere.

In a membership-driven congregation, maintaining membership is of the first importance. In a discipleship congregation, spiritual growth, service, and the well-being of the community of faith as a whole and all those who worship there are of the first importance. Sometimes the best thing we can do to empower individuals and families to meet their own spiritual needs and find venues for meaningful service is to refer them to another church where the biblical, theological, or practical focus might be more in tune with their needs at the time.

When we take seriously that all of life is a spiritual journey and that each of us is ultimately responsible for our own journey, we are free to end the destructive competition to gain and hold members that has plagued the Christian churches for far too long. A clear statement of beliefs provides the foundation for such spiritual freedom. The congregation's statement of beliefs is constitutive and thus essentially timeless. If the statement of beliefs changes, then the organization itself has become something else.

CLARIFYING YOUR VALUES

"I'm not only interested in what you believe, Pastor," he said. "I'm, frankly more interested in how you treat each other. My experience with the church has not always been very pleasant. I want to know if you're really as welcoming as you say you are."

I suspect that, truth be told, more people stay away from the church because we tolerate misbehavior than for any other reason. Often in workshops I will ask how many participants are businesspeople. Once they have identified themselves, I ask them to indicate by raising their hands if they agree with the following statement: "The church tolerates behaviors that business would never allow." I have yet to have business leaders disagree with that statement.

Why is this so? It seems to me that it is a question of values. As noted above, in a membership-driven congregation, gaining and maintaining members is a top—even if unspoken— value. To protect that value, patterns of behavior that in other settings would call for censure or discipline are tolerated. After all, to offend the offenders might cause them to leave. The chaplaincy model of ministry, rather than taking conflict head-on, encourages smoothing things over. Rude, demanding, controlling behavior is all too often tolerated when holding on to members is a controlling value in the congregation.

As a community of faith moves beyond membership to discipleship, it is important that it clearly define, affirm, and expect adherence to the values that shape community life and relationships. Values define common commitments with respect to how we live together.

A statement of values becomes a guide to the development of positive, healthy attitudes and behaviors and, when necessary, a benchmark against which our behaviors and attitudes can be held accountable. A public statement of values adopted by a community of faith represents a common commitment to a way of life. This is who we are; this is how we live.

At Prince of Peace we began with a list of fourteen values. This was a list, not a statement of our core values. We had found it helpful and important to surface all the values that commended themselves as vital to a discipleship congregation. Then, without rejecting any of them, we focused our attention on what seemed to be the key values, the ones that gave the greatest shape and cohesiveness to our vision of a Christian community of faith. The list of fourteen values was narrowed to a statement of five core values that we uphold as the attitudes and behaviors that embody our beliefs.

Prince of Peace Values
- Growing faith in Jesus Christ
- Compassion
- Personal integrity
- Innovation and excellence
- Community

Against this values checklist, we hold ourselves accountable for the quality of our life together and our personal growth as disciples of Christ.

James Collins and Jerry Porras, in their monumental work *Built to Last*,[18] have identified the presence of core beliefs and values as definitive for visionary companies. Visionary companies, such as Disney, Merck Pharmaceuticals, and Hewlett-Packard, are those that have stood the test of time and numerous changes in leadership and have still outperformed comparison companies. They have become significant cultures of innovation but hold all that they do accountable to their stated beliefs and values.

> Congregations that desire to be effective and vibrant ministries for generations to come will take the time to translate their beliefs into values.

One of the remarkable aspects of this study is the discovery that these companies may have very divergent rather than identical values—but they are true to themselves and successful because of it.

Congregations that desire to be effective and vibrant ministries for generations to come will take the time to translate their beliefs into values. Clearly articulated values give both leaders and followers clarity about how they are to journey together. Such a statement of values is only slightly more time-sensitive than the organization's statement of beliefs. If our values significantly change over time, it is likely that our beliefs have undergone reassessment and shift.

Leaders Articulate the Community's Defining Beliefs and Values

How do organizations establish such belief and values statements? It is a dialogical, but directed process. In all the cases I have studied, the leadership has articulated the core beliefs and identified the values that follow. The process begins with leaders leading.

Leaders begin with study. To articulate the beliefs and values of a local community that is part of a two-thousand-year-old religious tradition requires that the leader know that tradition, understand its development, have insight into when it was strong and true and when it was weak and false to itself. Biblical, theological, and historical training, which the laity normally do not have, lays a foundation from which the leader can begin to build the belief and value statements that will give identity and direction to the community of faith.

Also, leaders lead by prayerfully listening to God's people, watching the community at work, assessing and evaluating what they hear and see, and then stating the beliefs and values that, rooted in the traditions of the faith, seem most true and worthwhile for this particular community at this time.

The next step in the process is to share the core beliefs and values the leader has identified with the other leaders in the community. This is done trusting that the Spirit of Christ, given in baptism, is truly active in the disciples of Christ and that when we prayerfully listen to each other, we open ourselves to the voice of God in ways that we might not be able to hear by ourselves.

Once the leadership has agreed on the belief and value statements, the statements are then shared with the rest of the community. This can be done in a congregational meeting or forum or through focus groups. However they are communicated to the church, the message must be clear: these statements reflect the congregation's common beliefs and values. They will not necessarily reflect the positions of all of the community of believers gathered in that place. The clear statement of beliefs and values, however, gives people the opportunity to understand exactly what this particular community of faith is all about. If they cannot commit to the beliefs and values that define the congregation, they are free to leave. Or they are free to stick around and discover for themselves whether the beliefs and values the congregation lives by are capable of achieving and sustaining a high quality of Christian life together.

Normally, there will be a strong consensus as to the major beliefs and basic values of the congregation. People will go away from the meeting with a strong sense of identity and belonging. This is who we are; this is what we believe; this is how we act; this is what we do.

Not Everyone Will Get on Board—and That's OK

"I don't know if I can stay in this church," she said.

"Why not?" the council member asked.

"Well, I have a hard time accepting that our church's values allow each person to make their own decision on abortion."

"But we believe," the council member responded, "that the Holy Spirit guides the decision-making process of faithful Christians and that Christians can be faithful and hold a number of positions on that particular issue."

"That's the problem," she continued, "I don't."

When I overheard this conversation in a church I was visiting, I shared it with the pastor. He looked distressed at first but then said with a wry smile, "Well, I'd rather she left because she knows what we believe and doesn't agree than because she just got frustrated with the church or me for not taking a stand. Which," he continued, "is what usually happens in a lot of churches."

If the goal had been to maintain the membership of the congregation no matter what, then the conversation between the parishioner and the council member would have been quite distressing. The council member would probably have tried to smooth things over and avoid continued conflict. The woman might have gone on to threaten the withholding of offering or service until the church acceded to her position, and further attempts to mollify her would be made.

> When the goal is growth in responsible discipleship rather than holding members, letting people leave is a valid option. What is not an option is to compromise the beliefs and values of the congregation in the futile attempt to keep everyone happy.

But if the goal is growth in discipleship, then the council member would patiently explain the beliefs and values of the church that led it to its position on abortion and seek her understanding. Failing that, the council member would suggest a mutual process of discernment including a conversation with a pastor. The end result would be the decision to either stay in the congregation and prayerfully seek deeper understanding of the congregation's beliefs and values or leave the congregation and join another with beliefs and values closer to her own. When the goal is growth in responsible disciple-ship rather than holding members, letting people leave is a valid option. What is not an option is to compromise the beliefs and values of the congregation in the futile attempt to keep everyone happy.

Collins and Porras make it clear that, rather than compro-mise their core beliefs and values, visionary companies will actually sell off profitable subsidiaries. The issue is that of corporate identity and commitment to mission versus prof-itability. Visionary companies make it clear that, in conflicts like that, there is no real choice. And what is remarkable is that those companies of integrity that refuse to compromise and stay the course keeping their values intact don't have to worry about profitability! The church can do no less.

CULTURAL CHANGES REQUIRE MISSIONAL CLARITY

For all too many years my evangelical goals were to recruit and retain members within my congregation. At the time, the church growth movement was in full swing, and the end game was the growth of the Christian church through con-version and membership.

There is nothing wrong with conversion and consequent church affiliation by those who have been converted. After all, Christian mission involves witnessing to Jesus in such a way that the circle of faith is widened and Christian faith necessar-ily leads to involvement in a worshiping community of faith.

The problem, as I have argued earlier, is that the culture changed, and some of the assumptions undergirding the understanding of church affiliation as membership were no longer true. Of central importance was the subtle shift from an understanding of membership in terms of obligation to an understanding of membership in terms of prerogatives. This led, as mentioned earlier, to an internally focused ministry where the needs and demands of the membership largely replaced mission as the driving force of the church.

There have been other significant cultural shifts. For example, many of us grew up in a social context that was clearly based upon the Judeo-Christian ethic. We assumed that Christian ethical values would be reinforced by the public and private institutions around us. Monday through Friday the public school was an incubator for the ethical values taught at church on Sunday. The business community, media, government, and social service agencies were held accountable to a standard set of values that correlated well with those of the local congregation.

Our context has changed. One question that I often ask groups of Christian parents of young children is whether they believe that the moral values of their faith will be supported or reinforced in their children by the public schools. The answer is invariably no. This does not mean that the public schools are not valued by these same parents. It does mean, however, that we clearly live in a pluralistic society and people don't believe that our public schools will be "faith friendly." At best they are neutral, and at worst openly hostile, to faith-based moral values.

If we can no longer assume that the moral values of the church will be reinforced by the institutions around us, neither can we assume a significant level of general Christian religious awareness in the culture at large. Stemming from the notion of the village as extended family in days long past, the membership model assumed that certain faith-based moral values and ideas were commonly taught. The nuclear family was presumed to be the first place for this religious moral education, but the civic community was also expected to pass on the values and life truths that Christians held dear.

This is no longer the case. More and more, the people who come to our churches for the first time are people with little or no Christian memory, little or no understanding of what it means to be Christian. They come with a yearning of the heart, with needs and desires of one sort or another, but are largely unable to articulate them in the language of Christian faith and tradition. All of this leads to the conclusion that congregations must reevaluate their mission. It is no longer enough to simply "make members" and then assume that they will understand, let alone live, the life of faith. Membership does not equal faith-filled living. Once it may have, but it no longer does. Discipleship—committed, intelligent, faithful following of Christ in the world—is the marching order of the day.

MISSION EQUALS STRATEGIES FOR ENGAGING THE WORLD

Defining and clearly stating our mission as a particular community of faith is no longer optional. The mission of a congregation is its strategy for taking its beliefs and values into the world. This is the how of our engagement with the world God loves. The mission statement of a congregation describes how we shall interact as a community of faith with those outside the community.

At Prince of Peace, our mission statement is encapsulated in three words: *welcome, equip,* and *send.* These key words are at the heart of the mission statement:

> Prince of Peace exists to Welcome people to faith in Jesus Christ, Equip us for a faith that works in real life, and Send us into the world to make a difference in Jesus' Name.

The centrality of Christ is clear. Our methods and intention for engaging others are established. The focus of our relationships with one another within the community of faith is obvious. We will seek to be hospitable to everyone. Our ultimate goal is, by the power of the Holy Spirit, to make disciples of all. And we understand that as mobile as our society is and as young as our congregation is (our average age is thirty-one), we are not making disciples for our own congregation but for countless others to which our people will move and within which they will serve and grow.

A congregational mission statement must reflect and be consistent with its belief and values statements. The published mission statement is the first glimpse people have into the soul of the organization. It lets them know from the beginning what to expect. It is also a powerful tool for strategic planning and implementation. Everything the church does keys off the mission statement. The mission statement helps the congregation know what to say yes to and what to say no to in all of the opportunities presented to it for ministry and service.

What is your mission as a community of faith? Has it been clearly and publicly stated? Is it adequate to the work of love and justice God calls the church to? Does it engage the world or merely maintain the institution? Does it clearly express the expectation that those who identify with the congregation will seek to grow spiritually and serve faithfully?

You Can Expect More Than You Think

Some time ago I addressed a group of pastors and lay leaders on the topic of discipleship. During the question-and-answer period, one of the pastors pointedly stated his opinion: "We can't possibly expect this much of our members. Your discipleship model demands too much of people who are already doing too much."

Several clergy heads nodded in agreement, so I decided to take a risk and find out what the laypeople thought. "How many of you lay leaders," I asked, "think that your pastor expects too much of you spiritually?"

Not one hand went up! Of these deeply involved lay leaders, apparently no one thought their pastors were asking too much of them spiritually. Wherever I go, I keep asking the same question, and I keep getting the same answer. Clergy always assume they are asking too much and the laity say their pastors don't expect enough of them when it comes to spiritual growth. If the laity have any complaint, it is not that too much is expected, but that they need better mentoring and equipping in the spiritual practices that undergird the life of discipleship.

Disciples are eager to grow in their relationship to God in Jesus Christ. When their personal, spiritual life is affirmed, nurtured, and *related to the mission of the congregation*, wonderful things happen. A congregation that can accomplish this is one that is truly mission-driven.

CRAFTING A MISSION STATEMENT

A good place to begin crafting the mission statement that will move you forward is to develop a good sense of where you are now.[19] Listing what you are presently doing and then determining how these programs and activities relate to the congregation's beliefs and values will reveal gaps, inconsistencies, and untapped opportunities. Remember, the mission statement keys off the beliefs and values of the congregation, and the congregation's programs and activities will be keyed to the mission statement.

When finally formulated, the mission statement should be no more than three lines long, and you should be able to summarize it with three key words. This will give your ministry a sharp, clear focus that all who identify with the congregation will be able to understand and repeat.

Mission is proactive engagement with the world God loves. Therefore, the key words you choose to build your mission statement around must be action words—benchmarks against which faithful discipleship can be measured. The mission statement and the three key words that summarize it create a deep sense of shared purpose and direction.

A delightful tale from czarist Russia tells of a priest who was walking along minding his own business when a royal guard stopped him at gunpoint. The guard demanded, "What is your name? Why are you here, and where are you going?"

The priest gazed quizzically at the soldier and then asked, "How much do they pay you to do this work?"

The soldier, somewhat taken aback, replied, "Why, three kopeks a month."

"I'll pay you thirty kopeks a month if you will stop me every week and ask me these same questions," the priest said.

That's what a good mission statement does. It keeps us thinking about who we are, why we are here, and where we are going.

Mission statements translate beliefs and values into a strategy to engage the world. They are outward-looking, and what you see when you look out will depend on where you are. That is why "one size fits all" mission statements are not possible. Each congregation has its own social location and context and needs a mission statement that responds to the realities and needs of its own neighborhood.

> A good mission statement keeps us thinking about who we are, why we are here, and where we are going.

Unlike statements of belief and values, mission statements are somewhat time-sensitive. Even though the beliefs and values of a community of faith may not change, the context for its mission will. As the context changes significantly, strategies for engaging the world in the name of Jesus will also need to change. Mission statements need to be reviewed over against the context of mission on a regular basis. Such a review might well lead to a new mission statement and the "reinvention" and revitalization of the congregation's ministry and mission.

Successful, vital businesses are reinventing themselves every three to five years. In contrast, students of the American church report that congregations typically reinvent themselves every thirty to forty years! Leith Anderson, senior pastor of Wooddale Church in Eden Prairie, Minnesota, argues persuasively that with the fast pace of social, demographic, economic, and technological change in America, congregations ought to be "reinventing" themselves about every seven years.[20]

The very idea that a congregation would need to reinvent itself is foreign to most church leaders. The reinventing of other institutions and organizations, however, demonstrates a dramatic revitalizing effect when an organization reconnects with its changing context of "business." Momentum is created, change is focused, clarity of purpose is restored, and a renewed commitment to the "customer" sparks innovation and effectiveness. The Christian church needs nothing less.

Once you have crafted a mission statement that boldly and clearly states your strategy for engagement, you will need to share it broadly with the congregation. Recall the Prince of Peace mission statement: *Prince of Peace exists to Welcome people to faith in Jesus Christ, Equip us for a faith that works in real life, and Send us into the world to make a difference in Jesus' Name.* In order to keep the mission front and center, we even structure our worship around the three key words that summarize our mission statement: *welcome, equip,* and *send.* Over and over again, using creative and innovative formats, our six large video screens communicate our mission and our commitment to the marks of discipleship.

Leaders must use every means available to get and keep the mission statement before the people. Keep in mind John Kotter's statement that leaders typically under-communicate. When you think you have run the message into the ground, you most likely will have just begun to communicate effectively. Leaders should definitely memorize the mission statement, and those who identify with the congregation should be encouraged to do the same. Post it in obvious places. Print it in the Sunday bulletin and the church newsletter. Add it to the letterhead of your stationery. Use it intentionally in planning and evaluation. It won't be long before everyone in the church has no difficulty explaining to any who ask what the community of faith is all about.

MISSION-DRIVEN MEANS VISION-LED

If the life of the church is driven by its mission, then it will be led by its vision. Vision is a clear picture of the desired present and the preferred future. Vision is the end toward which mission drives. All of the various programs and ministries in a congregation are focused through the lens of the mission statement and directed toward the realization of the vision.

How does a vision emerge within a community of faith? Does it simply well up out of the congregation, or do leaders have the responsibility to initiate the vision? According to George Barna, "Vision is a clear and precise mental portrait of a preferable future, imparted by God to his chosen servants, based on an accurate understanding of God, self and circumstances."[21] In other words, vision comes from God through the leader of a community. It emerges out of the depths of the leader's own discipleship.

Vision is a compelling picture of what the community of faith would look like if it was truly effective in living out its beliefs and values through its mission. The vision for Prince of Peace is simple:

> Our vision is of a thriving church that changes lives and leads the culture by growing, through the power of the Holy Spirit, 10,000 passionate followers of Jesus Christ in every generation.

The implications of this simple statement of the desired outcome of our mission are multiple. We believe that we cannot achieve this vision by our own efforts. Thus we are constantly seeking partnerships and cooperative alliances with other like-minded organizations. For example, our vision is clearly cross-generational. In order to realize the vision, we have begun to partner with the Ebenezer Society, a local ministry to the elderly. We regularly bring children and youth to the larger campus on which we are located. The Ebenezer Society brings the elderly. Together we are developing a remarkable intergenerational ministry that builds significant, life-transforming relationships between the generations. Since we share with the Ebenezer Society beliefs, values, and a strong commitment to the gospel, this partnership fits squarely within our mission and vision. Together we are realizing the vision in ways we could not do alone.

In a similar manner we have partnered with Pastor David Stark and his colleagues around the "Life Keys" model of gift assessment. Passionate followers of Jesus Christ know that they are God's agents in the world. As they identify and develop their gifts, talents and personality traits and get connected in activities that match their skills, interests, and passions, they are more effective in transformational service. This relationship also fits well with our vision and mission.

With an aggressive, but realistic vision, leaders are encouraged to seek out partnerships, alliances, and relationships with like-minded organizations that extend their reach and increase their effectiveness. Clear vision releases imagination, creativity, and innovation in mission.

"Pastor Mike, we are here to see how Prince of Peace can be involved in the significant social ministry of affordable housing," she said. "Most people think of affordable housing as strictly for the poor, the welfare family. But it's not," she continued. "Affordable housing makes it possible for single parents, the elderly, and the recent college graduate to find worthwhile places to live in our area. And," she said with a smile, "it fits our vision and our mission. We can make a different community and world in Jesus' name by making such housing available for all generations."

> Vision aligns the passions of all kinds of people around common goals.

She had me! She knew that the question wasn't whether this or that was a good idea, but whether it fit the mission and vision of Prince of Peace. She had already filtered her idea through that question and the connection was obvious.

This is the power of vision. Vision aligns the passions of all kinds of people around common goals. Vision unites the hearts and efforts of many in realizing today as much as possible of the future we are moving toward.

It bears repeating: vision emerges from the spiritual depths of the leader's own discipleship. The importance, therefore, of leaders who practice the marks of discipleship and tend seriously to their own spiritual lives must be underscored. Out of the "divine chemistry" of the leader's relationship with God comes a vision for the future of the community of faith.

"Honey, I have to share with you what I believe God is calling me to do," I said to my wife, Christine.

"Unless you think I am totally off base," I continued, "I'll take it to the church council and then to the staff. If they don't buy it, don't worry, we won't have to move, because I'll plant another church in this area!" Then, I shared my vision for a community of discipleship and we prayed together. Chris confirmed my vision, and I began to share it with the leadership.

CRAFTING AND CASTING A VISION IS A LEADERSHIP PROCESS

The first glimpse of the vision belongs to the leader. Out of his or her ongoing prayer, Bible study, and reflection on the community and its needs comes a compelling picture of what the church might be and do in this place, at this time, with these people. When the picture has enough specificity to commend itself to others, it is time to draw the community's leaders into the process. As the leader first listened to God, now it is time to listen to the leaders that serve God's church.

A formal letter of invitation to a large circle of significant leaders asking them to attend an orientation meeting is a good place to begin. At the meeting, the senior leader invites attendees to participate in a congregational study process that will set the stage for a thoughtful and prayerful assessment of the vision that he or she feels called to share with them.

The study process will look carefully at the congregation's internal demographics as well as at the external demographics of the areas the congregation is presently serving and hopes to serve in the future. Present programs and activities will be looked at in the light of the demographic analysis. It may take months to gather the date, share it, evaluate it, and reflect upon what it might mean for the ministry and mission of the congregation, but when the task is done, the group of leaders will have a clear context within which to hear, consider, and, one hopes, "catch" the leader's vision.

When the congregational study is complete, the senior leader simply and prayerfully sets the vision before the leadership group. Breakout groups—in which the senior leader does not participate—provide opportunities for frank and open discussion. A plenary session in which the breakout groups share their insights and concerns with the larger group provides the senior leader with an opportunity to listen and learn. Rarely will there be unquestioned commitment to the vision in its first rendition.

The senior leader listens, takes copious notes, asks clarifying questions, and calls another leadership meeting two weeks down the road. In the interim, the senior leader prayerfully revisits the original vision in the light of the leadership group's response. Two weeks later, the leader presents a revised vision to the same group. The process repeats itself: breakout groups, reporting back to the whole group, more listening, note taking, and questioning. The leader takes as many weeks as is needed to develop a vision that excites, motivates, and claims the loyalty of the community's leaders.

Finally, the vision is brought to the church board for adoption. The support of staff and lay ministry leaders who did not participate in the visioning group is enlisted. And then the vision is shared with the entire congregation. Again, what may feel like over-communication is necessary to get the greatest possible congregational "ownership" for the vision.

Of the four documents we have described in this chapter, the vision statement is the most time-sensitive. The future has a way of rushing toward us when we have more clearly defined it. A congregation's vision will require modification, adaptation, perhaps replacement every two to three years if the church is to remain responsive to its context and the God who calls it into mission.

I regularly drive past congregations that in previous generations had a vibrant and effective ministry. Now, however, that ministry is on its last legs. Not only has the worshiping community dwindled—and with it, most of its resources—but the congregation is no longer effectively, if at all, engaging the larger community where it is located. This is rarely the failure of care or hard work. It is almost always the failure of vision. Yesterday's reality is not today's—let alone tomorrow's. A clear-sighted vision backed by dynamic mission strategies can capture the imaginations and energies of God's people and send them on the way to God's future.

QUESTIONS FOR PRAYERFUL REFLECTION

1. What are the bottom-line beliefs that provide the bedrock on which you and your congregation stand? How are these beliefs communicated and reinforced?

2. What are the fundamental values that govern personal and corporate attitudes and behaviors in your congregation? Are people held accountable to these values?

3. What is the mission statement of your congregation?

Does it powerfully integrate your beliefs and values into strategies for engaging the world outside the church?

4. What is the preferred future for your congregation? Is this vision compelling to both leadership and worshipers?

5. If you have belief and values statements as well as mission and vision statements, how are they communicated and used to guide the life of the congregation?

6. If you do not have belief and values statements or mission and vision statements, do you feel it would be important to craft them? If no, why not? If yes, how would you go about doing so?

MISSION IS PROACTIVE
ENGAGEMENT WITH THE
WORLD GOD LOVES.

7

Beyond committees to ministry teams

"**W**hen we left your Changing Church Conference, we were so excited," a pastor from an inner-city church said. "Blow up our committees! Well, we took that idea back to the congregation, and we did it. We blew up our committees and established ministry teams with clear objectives for service. That was four months ago. At that time," she continued, "we had a total of 25 volunteers. Now we have 125! And it's incredible!"

On the other hand . . .

I'll never forget my first stewardship committee meeting at Prince of Peace. The topic on the agenda was the annual pledge drive. After more than an hour of a spirited sharing of ideas, the group was unanimous about taking a particular approach to the pledge drive.

Then the chair spoke, "So, what do we do now, Pastor Mike?"

"Well," I naively replied, "we implement the program and inform the church of our plans." Silence filled the room, and I knew that I had done or said something unnerving.

"Can we really do that?" he asked. "In the past we always had to report to the executive committee of the council and get their approval before we could do anything."

"Are we going to spend more than the amount budgeted for us?" I asked.

"No. In fact, we'll probably spend less," he replied.

"Then surely we can just do it. I can't imagine that the executive committee would want to hold us up. We've had some great thinking here tonight. So let's just do it," I said.

Then something delightful and empowering happened in that conference room. The chair grinned and looked at the other members of the committee. They grinned back as he said, "I'd like to receive a motion to implement the steward-ship plan set before us."

The motion was quickly made, seconded, and unani-mously passed.

Later, I learned that one of our best givers had previously resigned from the stewardship committee. His reason was not that he found it boring, nor that he no longer cared about the stewardship of the congregation.

"Pastor," he said, "I couldn't stand it. Every time we got excited about a stewardship project, we were stopped in our tracks. We couldn't do anything. We had to wait for some-one else to think it through and then give us permission to act. If I ran my business that way, not only would I eventu-ally go out of business, but my best people would leave first."

Most churches are structured for control, not mission. The average church council is a group of sixteen or more members, each of whom is the chair of a committee. The role of the council is to review the actions of the committees, determine whether they serve the interests of the congregation, and then affirm or reject those proposals. In short, the council receives reports from committees and, on important issues and plans, often rethinks and redoes the committee's work. It is no wonder that leaders from the business community, social service sector, and government are unwilling to serve on many congregations' committees.

No one wants to give time and energy to projects they care about but over which they finally have little say and less control. George Barna has said that time is the new currency. We value things more by our willingness to give time to them than by our willingness to spend money on them. The structure of most congregations devalues time and overvalues position.

FROM CHURCH COUNCIL
TO CHURCH BOARD

Discipleship congregations are willing to adopt a governance system that authorizes rather than gets in the way of disciples in mission. In many congregations, this means replacing the council-committee structure with a board–ministry team structure.

Unlike a church council that is actively involved in the administration of the church, a church board functions like the architect of a building. The architect determines where the heating source will be located in the building and may even recommend the appropriate type of energy for the heating and cooling system. But he or she does not operate and maintain the heating and cooling system itself. That is the job of the maintenance-facilities service personnel.

A church board is responsible for the *governance* of the congregation, not the *operational administration* of the congregation. The board establishes policies, approves the overall budget, sets fiscal and personnel practices, and adopts the vision for the congregation. The actual day-to-day operations of the church belong to the staff and the various ministry teams of the congregation. The board, in effect, sets the boundaries within which the ministry operates. The disciples—beginning with the staff—determine the play of the game within those boundaries.

At Prince of Peace, the board has nine members with full voice and vote. The senior pastor serves as one of the nine. A tenth member of the board is the past president, who has voice but no vote. His or her participation guarantees the presence of corporate memory. An eleventh member serves as legal counsel; in this litigious age, legal counsel is a must for congregations. As with the tenth member, this position is a matter of voice without vote.

Board members are selected by a ballot of affirmation. The nominating ministry team surfaces individuals who have the ability to see the big picture. They look for individuals who will bring a balance of expertise to the board and who have been identified as having the gift of leadership. This is an imperfect process, but with a careful description of the kinds of expertise desired, the nominating team has a good chance to succeed.

Once the nominating team has come up with an adequate number of names and established a priority ranking the individuals selected, the process goes internal. The staff are asked to comment on their experience with those identified as potential leaders. In smaller congregations, the pastor(s) will be more likely to have direct experience of nominated leaders and can use his or her judgment as to how they have fulfilled leadership responsibilities or participated in ministry or service projects.

Each potential board member is examined with respect to his or her financial stewardship. We are not concerned with dollar amounts but with the relationship between what is given and one's potential to give. A single mother with a limited income who tithes is just as eligible for election to the board, if she can demonstrate the appropriate leadership skills, as a highly paid executive of a Fortune 500 company.

The principle is clear: board members are disciples who are charged with leading a discipleship congregation. Disciples understand the need for disciplined, habitual giving—it is a mark of discipleship.

Paul's words to the Corinthian Christians are worth repeating: "For if the eagerness is there, the gift is acceptable according to what one has—not according to what one does not have" (2 Corinthians 8:12). Thus, a potential board member who is "upside down" economically is not expected to give as much as one whose salary is large and secure. The accountability of board members is rooted in the grace of our most generous God.

Board members are elected for three-year terms and can succeed themselves once without a necessary yearlong absence from service. The board structure empowers disciples for ministry, and as a result, board members cannot serve as chairpersons of ministry teams. The board governs, the staff administers, the disciples do ministry.

DISCOURAGEMENT GUARANTEED

Imagine the usual system of governance and control in most congregations. The church council is made up of (1) the executive committee, (2) designated staff, and (3) the chairpersons of various committees. The design is intended to enhance both communication and decision making. Unfortunately, however, it rarely works that way.

Imagine that system from the perspective of a lay disciple who has a creative, innovative idea that she believes will serve the mission of the church. If this person is not on the inside of the system, not a member of the council or a committee, she will probably go to the pastor—or one of the pastors in a multiple-staff situation—and share her idea. The pastor will listen politely but finally refer her to the appropriate chair of the appropriate committee. The chairperson will also listen politely and promise to get her idea on the agenda of the next committee meeting—which may not be meeting again for one or more months.

At the next committee meeting, the idea will be discussed and, if it isn't rejected out of hand because of budget or other constraints, will be referred to the church council for further discussion. At the next council meeting, the idea will be presented with the committee's recommendation, considered, and finally subjected to one of several possible actions. The council may (1) table the idea for future consideration, (2) refer it back to the committee for another go-around, (3) reject it as either inappropriate or "outside of the budget," or (4) vote to accept it and send it back to the committee for implementation.

By this time, the outcome hardly matters to the person who came up with the idea. Whatever the council decides to do, the disciple with a passion for ministry and a creative idea to share has already heard no three times. The first no came from the pastor or staff member who said he couldn't respond to the idea officially and referred her to the "appropriate" committee. The second no came from the chair of the committee who was unable to respond in any coherent way to the suggestion and could only offer to put it on the agenda of the next meeting. The third no came from the committee that made it clear that, no matter how great the idea was, it had no authority to implement it and would have to refer it on to church council. More often than not, that turns into a fourth no when the council either refers the idea back to the original committee for more discussion or simply rejects it. Should the council finally vote to accept and implement the idea, it will need to work its way back down through the committee structure before it sees the light of day. By that time, anywhere from three to six months or more will have passed and the passion that gave birth to the idea in the first place will probably have faded. The result: one more discouraged disciple. Discipleship congregations simply cannot tolerate a structure that discourages passion, impedes creativity, stifles innovation, and simply takes too much time to get things done. They need to equip leaders with the skills and resources necessary for particular ministries and then authorize those closest to the ministry to make and implement appropriate decisions.

Not Just Another Name for Committees

A rose by any other name, it has been said, smells the same. Ministry teams, however, are not just another name for committees. A ministry team functions on an "as needed" basis *to get things done.* Ministry teams come into existence in order to meet a need. Once that need is met, they no longer meet. There can be, and certainly are, ongoing ministry teams, but even those teams meet, disband for a while, and then regather when necessary in order to accomplish specific goals and objectives. Ministry teams are designed to accomplish something.

At the end of my talk, a young woman stood to ask a question I often hear: "I still don't get it," she said. "Just what is the difference between a ministry team and a committee?"

"Well, let me ask you all a question," I replied. "You are all lay leaders in your congregations. So tell me, how many of you would be willing to serve on another committee?"

My question generated the response I expected—only those over age fifty-five raised their hands. People were clearly uncomfortable with the question. As committed lay leaders, they wanted to serve their congregations in whatever way needed. As folks who had been around a while, they knew the frustration of working with a committee structure.

"For those of you who didn't raise your hands," I went on, "let me ask you why you didn't."

A young woman, who appeared to be in her mid-thirties, blurted out, "It's simple. Committees don't do anything! They just talk and talk and talk!"

Looking at her I asked, "But if you were asked to join a team of people to accomplish a specific goal that you cared about, in a given period of time, would you do it?"

"In a heartbeat," she responded.

Turning to the woman who had asked the original question, I said, "That is the difference between a committee and a ministry team."

> Teams harness more energy, see from more vantage points, and create more momentum than committees.

Teams harness more energy, see from more vantage points, and create more momentum than committees. Energy, a variety of perspectives, and momentum maximize the effectiveness of any ministry. A team, of course, is not always necessary. There are some jobs that can be handled by an individual. Those, however, will be the exception, not the rule. If a ministry is worth doing, chances are that it will be best accomplished by teaming.

Getting Started with Teams

Discipleship congregations, eager for the power surge that comes when passionate Christians are authorized and resourced for ministry and mission, are deliberate in creating a team-based culture. Education is important. The congregation needs to know the nature and scope of the change and the benefits of the change to the ministry and mission of the church. Various methods help to create a healthy climate for teams to function: a onetime brief introduction to the team concept and its benefits when the community has gathered for worship, direct mailing, newsletter articles, and staff who are committed to the change and take every opportunity to explain the ministry team concept to people.

Whenever a ministry need arises, it is important to quickly form a team, assign a team leader, establish clear goals and objectives, and set a time line. How to meet established goals and objectives within the time frame allowed is the responsibility of the team. Set them loose, and watch the creativity flow.

As a transitional strategy while you move from a committee-based to a team-based model, consider transforming your present committees into teams. First, change the name of the groups and publish them broadly. Second, invite present "committee" members to become "team" members. Replace any who opt out with high-energy volunteers. Make it clear to all that there is no longer a "chairperson" in charge, but that there is a "team leader" authorized to make decisions. Third, ask team members to identify three major goals for their team and set a time frame for accomplishing them. Remind them to key their goals off the mission and vision of the church. Fourth, ask the team to inform you when they decide to stop meeting because the job is done. Fifth, let them know that you trust them to do what they are called to do but that you will also hold them accountable to the tasks they have taken on. Work with them to develop realistic mileposts and benchmarks to evaluate their success. And finally, recognize their accomplishments and celebrate them as a congregation.

In a discipleship congregation, ministry teams are seen as microcosms of the larger congregational culture. Teams—no matter what their specific ministry goals and objectives might be—are garden plots for spiritual growth and the experience of a caring, committed community. Teams are made up of people with a shared passion, a common commitment, and clear ends in mind. As such, they are marvelous opportunities for spiritual growth through Bible study, prayer, and conversation. Every team meeting must begin with scripture and prayer. Ideally all team meetings will provide an opportunity for all team members to "check in" with one another.

The morning was just beginning. We had come with our hammers and saws. The lumber was piled up before us. Now the Habitat for Humanity team leader was telling us what we needed to accomplish that day. Having laid out the plan and established individual and subteam responsibilities, he opened the Bible and read from the Gospel of John. Then, he shared briefly about what was going on in his life and asked for prayer. He also asked the assembled team if any of them had any prayer requests. Some did, and they shared briefly. Then the team leader led us in a time of common prayer. Only after that did we get to work. That is a picture of a ministry team in action.

At Prince of Peace, board members bring Bibles to their meetings. The meetings begin with a Bible study, led by the senior pastor, focusing on leadership. Board meetings last only ninety minutes and, when the agenda is full—as it usually is—I have been tempted to drop the leadership Bible study. The board members quickly rejected that idea. Why? Because the business of the church must serve the ministry of the church. The ministry of Price of Peace is to grow disciples—and that begins and continues with our leaders. When a board rushes through its devotional time to "get at the real agenda," it is easy to forget why the board is meeting in the first place. The real agenda of the church is its spiritual agenda. (I have yet to meet a church leader who serves on the board because she or he just wanted another opportunity to do business.) The church board is a ministry team in its own right with all of the dynamics described above.

A teaming culture is also a learning organization. In his groundbreaking book *The Fifth Discipline*,[22] Peter Senge identifies the major characteristics of a learning organization. Of key importance is the fact that a learning organization is not afraid of failure. In fact, learning organizations understand that learning means risk. Taking risks means that sometimes our identified objectives are not accomplished. We fail. In the long run, however, that may be the best thing that could have happened. Remember, in a discipleship congregation, failure is not failure if you learn from it. Ministry teams may fail, but if failure is looked upon as an opportunity to learn and grow, it is a "redeemed" failure.

> In a discipleship congregation, failure is not failure if you learn from it.

The fear of failure is the single greatest danger for new ministry teams. When we fear failure, we look for "experts" to give us the answers. When we are afraid to fail, we are not open to new ideas and risky enterprises. When the specter of failure haunts us, we significantly limit our opportunities to learn and grow. To create a healthy, team-based congregational culture, leadership must put the right perspective on "failure."

In a team-based culture, the sharing of knowledge and the practical wisdom that comes from experience is encouraged and expected. The tragedy of committee-based systems is that they encourage silos, separated ministries that do not share and may even compete with one another. Sadly, in the committee-based model, different areas of ministry often replicate each other's failures simply because what was learned from hard experience in one area of ministry is not shared with other areas of ministry. Discipleship ministries, however, are willing—indeed, they are eager—to share successes and failures with one another for the sake of the mission of the church.

The Annual Meeting: Making It Work

"How many of you look forward to annual meetings?" I asked the approximately 150 pastors from a wide variety of denominational affiliations. To no one's surprise, not a single hand was raised. Instead, there was a collective groan.

Discipleship congregations still have annual meetings. Unlike most annual meetings, however, they aren't just constitutional requirements attended by only a few and finished as quickly as possible. The annual meeting in a discipleship congregation is shaped to serve the mission and vision of the community of faith.

Annual meetings in a discipleship congregation are concerned with much more than approving budgets, receiving reports, and electing officers. First and foremost they are about the spiritual life of the church. Worship, therefore, is first on the agenda at the annual meetings of discipleship congregations. The annual meeting is one more focused opportunity for disciples to grow deeper in the faith.

The necessary business of the annual meeting should be accomplished before the meeting is held. The budget and significant ministry issues should be frankly and carefully discussed in multiple open forums scheduled at times when as many worshipers as possible can attend. This opens the process to the entire congregation, not just those who have an ax to grind or who are single-issue constituents. By scheduling multiple open forums on significant ministry and missional issues in the weeks before the annual meeting, it is more likely that anything important that congregational leaders may have missed will be caught. After these forums have given people ample opportunity to hear and be heard, the annual meeting can focus on the business agenda in a way that will truly serve the mission of the church.

Most of our annual meetings miss a great opportunity to communicate with the larger congregation. Dr. Leonard Sweet, an insightful observer of the American church, noted in a gathering in Los Angeles that one of the major cultural shifts of our time is the move *from legislation to participation.* People are less willing to attend legislative meetings than ever before. Meaningful participation is what counts for more and more of the people who worship in our churches. Schedule the annual meeting within worship itself, and those who are not interested in the legislative process will find themselves participating in it in a way that invites their commitment to the mission and vision of the church in deeply significant ways.

No matter how it is structured, the annual meeting should:

• Worship first
• Next, acknowledge, affirm, and celebrate the significant achievements of the past year
• Then, lift up the challenges before the congregation in the coming year
• And finally, do the business required to meet those challenges

Annual meetings need not bore people to tears. When the business of the church is conducted in the midst of celebration, when it is done in the context of a great vision for the future of the community of faith, when the mundane business of budgets and elections is seen in the light of the divine call to the congregation, be prepared for a power surge. Exciting things will happen.

Questions for Prayerful Reflection

1. Is your congregation committee-based or ministry team-based? If committee-based, what would be most exciting and most frightening about "blowing up your committees"?

2. What ministry teams could your congregation use now? Are there leaders and volunteers available? What kind of a ministry team pilot project could you develop?

3. Is your congregation organized for control or for mission? How do you know? If control is overly important, what do you need to do to let go and focus on mission?

4. What are the respective strengths and weaknesses of church councils and church boards as governance structures? Which do you have? Is it working? Why or why not?

5. Do your annual meetings work? If not, why not? What could you do to release a power surge through them?

THE BOARD GOVERNS,
THE STAFF ADMINISTRATES,
THE DISCIPLES DO MUCH.

8 Developing Leaders for the church and the world

THE NUMBER ONE PRIORITY FOR LEADERS

When it comes to leadership, on the nurture-versus-nature argument I come down on the side of nurture. Effective leaders are not born; they are made. There are identifiable skills and perspectives, work and relational habits, disciplines and practices that make good leaders. These are transferable skills, teachable practices, and learnable habits. Under the wise mentoring of an accomplished leader, novice leaders flourish and grow. When one considers the immediate and future needs of the church in ministry and mission, it is not an overstatement to say that undertaking such mentoring and developing new leaders is a leader's top priority.

"I am interested in how I got here," she said. It was the first meeting of our Young Leaders' Forum.

"Well," I began, "you were identified by another leader in the church as a person who had already demonstrated leadership qualities in a particular area of ministry. I don't have that list in front of me or I could tell you exactly which area it was in."

"That's OK," she said, "I just wanted to know why I was here."

At Prince of Peace, the Young Leaders' Forum was our first deliberate attempt to seek out, identify, and develop potential leaders. There were three clear objectives for this group experience:

- to connect young leaders with one another
- to nurture their capacity for leadership
- to provide me with an opportunity to get to know them and to share with them the vision and mission that was calling for their leadership

The first objective was based on two clear assumptions. First, we believed—and still believe—that leaders grow best within a team of other leaders. Second, we believed—and still do—that connecting people and encouraging spiritual relationships is essential for a dynamic community of faith. By providing an opportunity for a shared, focused learning experience, we provided a context in which both leadership skills and personal relationships could grow.

The second objective was tackled from two vantage points. First, at the beginning of each meeting I led a short Bible study on various leadership-related themes. The Bible study set the ground for the night's topic, which was then introduced by one of the congregation's acknowledged leaders. These leaders were people of various ages who represented a variety of vocational backgrounds and experiences in the different ministries of the church. Each of them had integrated her or his faith into the dynamics of daily living.

By having a variety of leaders share their perspective and experience with the Young Leaders' Forum, we created a team approach that exposed participants to a wide range of effective leadership styles.

The third objective gave focus to the whole enterprise. My sharing of the vision and mission that formed the context for their future leadership made clear to them that leadership is not an end in itself. Rather, it serves the higher call of God. The forum also provided me with an opportunity, as senior pastor, to meet and get to know the emerging leadership of the church. As much as I might like to, given the size of our congregation, it is impossible for me to develop close relationships with all of the many leaders who serve God and the people of God at Prince of Peace. Still, connection is important. The Young Leaders' Forum connects us at the level of our common purpose, common direction, and common commitments to discipleship.

At Prince of Peace, we have what might be called an "authorization model" of leadership. We identify leaders, train them, provide them with the skills and resources they need to be effective, and then get out of their way. They are "authorized" to lead. We hold them accountable for results but do not micromanage them. In such a culture, the senior leadership must know frontline leadership well enough to be comfortable that everyone is on the same wavelength. By framing the mentoring process of our Young Leader's Forum within the vision and mission of the congregation, we know we are all headed in the same direction.

ON-THE-JOB TRAINING

Father Bill Cunningham is quoted as saying, "Leadership is about taking people to places where they have never dared to go."[23] The Christian church—through its leaders—is called to do just that, to "take people places where they have never dared to go."

The vision of the kingdom of God stretches our imagination and calls us toward God's future. It is incumbent upon every church to raise up leaders who share this vision with passion. The first step, as I have tried to explain in this book, is to embrace discipleship. Congregations where everyone is encouraged to practice the marks of discipleship are congregations rooted in the practices of the spiritual life. Vision and passion spring from the disciplines of prayer, worship, holy reading, spiritual friendships, and the practice of generosity. The marks of discipleship are the seedbed of passionate, visionary leadership.

> It is critical that discipleship congregations develop procedures and programs to identify and train new leaders.

It is critical that discipleship congregations develop procedures and programs to identify and train new leaders. But that is not enough. Programs such as the Young Leaders' Forum must lead to practical on-the-job training opportunities where leadership is practiced on the front lines of ministry, where leaders are mentored, and where experience becomes the best teacher.

The discipleship model of leadership development mirrors the relationship between Jesus of Nazareth and his disciples. Jesus took time with his disciples. He taught them to pray, opened the scriptures to them, and lived among them the life he expected from them. He challenged them, supported them, and forgave them when they failed to understand or to act up to his example. After teaching them the message and the mission he "gave them authority" and sent them out two by two to preach, teach, and heal (Matthew 10; Mark 6:7-13; Luke 9:1-6; 10:1-12). Call it on-the-job-training with an "authorization model" ministry.

From the moment he called people to be disciples, Jesus began an intentional process of teaching, modeling, and mentoring that left the infant church with a dynamic core of leadership that began to replicate itself as the church spread across the ancient world. Discipleship congregations continue this intentional process.

No leadership development process is complete without an evaluation component. The development process must include evaluation, encouragement, and challenge. New leaders often know gratifying success in leadership. They also frequently fail. Some things go well, others not so well. Mistakes are made, goals missed, and opportunities lost. But, as I've said several times before, failure is not failure when we learn from it. Ongoing evaluation allows us to learn from our good and bad experiences.

Mentors need to help new leaders establish realistic milestones and benchmarks against which they can judge their effectiveness. Giving feedback is important as long as it is not carping criticism but creative critique that helps young leaders reflect on their performance. Teaching novice leaders how to ask for and receive feedback from other leaders and from those who follow them is also a key factor in leadership development. Leadership is not an ego game, and developing leaders need to learn how to seek, not fear, constructive feedback—even when it is painful.

Dr. Lee Griffin once told me, "All life learning comes from pain. Unfortunately, not all pain leads to learning." The deciding factor here is not the depth or breadth of the pain but our willingness to reflect upon it. When we step back from our pain, embarrassment, or confusion for a time of careful and prayerful reflection, we put some objective space between ourselves and the immediacy of our feelings. Reflecting on our experiences means that for the moment we are not caught up in them. In a very real sense, we transcend them in order to translate our pain into learning. Leaders learn this lesson over time. They also learn that this kind of focused reflection happens best in conversations with a caring and experienced mentor.

"This has been the most painful experience I think I've ever been through," said the leader of a ministry team. Things had seemed to be going well, but then bitter internal conflict had erupted. The project the team had been working on, and for which he felt responsible, was abandoned, and he became the object of vicious gossip. "I don't think I ever want to lead a team again."

"Well," his pastor gently replied, "that is one possible response. But think for a moment. Isn't leadership about risk—even risking ourselves—for the sake of something worthwhile? Let me ask you a question," the pastor continued. "If you were to do it over again, what would you do differently?"

The young man thought for a moment. "The only thing that comes to mind is that I would have been much more careful about whom I recruited to be on the team. And I would have taken more time to listen to them as well."

"That's good," his pastor replied. "Making sure you have the right people with the right skills and the right attitude is important to the success of any ministry team. And then being available to listen to them, to answer their questions and listen to their advice, suggestions, and concerns helps them take ownership of the mission. Now, tell me," he continued, "what did you do really well?"

"For a while we really understood our mission. In the beginning, I talked a lot about our mission and why it was important. We talked together and shared ideas. We were passionate about it. We were really accomplishing a lot. But after a while, instead of talking together, sharing ideas, and encouraging one another, we seemed to start bickering."

He stopped to think. "It all ended when we seemed to lose sight of why we were together in the first place. Maybe that's the greatest lesson in this for me. When you lose sight of your mission, your purpose, it's a lot easier to see the short-comings of those around you."

Leadership is hard work, which is exactly what that young man learned. But he did learn. How tragic it would be if that learning was lost to the church. Encouraging young leaders to get back in the saddle after having fallen off the horse—and providing opportunities for them to do so—is an important part of responsible mentoring.

Getting beyond failure does not mean pretending that it didn't happen, nor does it mean pretending that the pain of it was inconsequential. It does mean, however, accepting both our brokenness and God's infinite restoring grace. Discipleship leaders will simply not allow failure to go untransformed into learning. Getting beyond failure means giving thanks for what we have learned through failure. Peter may never have learned the depth of Christ's forgiveness without the failures of Holy Week. Failure and conflict are harsh teachers, but they are teachers. The key is to not get stuck in them but to learn from them and get back to work.

> Getting beyond failure means giving thanks for what we have learned through failure.

With the young man in our story, it would not have been wise at that time to ask him to lead an unstable or conflicted team, but neither would it have been wise to remove him from a leadership role altogether. Those who mentor young leaders look for appropriate leadership opportunities. In the case of this young man, that meant finding him a more modest leadership role in a smoothly functioning ministry team. His pastor did exactly that. As a result, the young leader helped successfully achieve the team's goal and had a positive leadership experience. He was, as it were, back on the horse.

DISCIPLESHIP BEYOND THE BOUNDARIES OF THE CHURCH

Another often overlooked value of nurturing Christian leaders for service in the church is that we are also training men and women for Christian leadership in the world outside the church. When such leaders are developed and exercise their skills in the larger community, the church is no longer simply reacting to the world but proactively helping to shape it.

In order for the church to fully accept the task of training leaders for service beyond the congregation, it needs to be clear about the boundaries of discipleship: there are none! There is no place where a Christian does not live as a Christian. There is no place where a Christian is not called to participate in God's love for the world. Discipleship takes place wherever disciples find themselves.

"Pastor," she said with conviction, "your idea of mission is too small. I'm not called to serve in the church. I know that God has called me to serve in the school district. Surely you would acknowledge that God can call me to work in society and not just in the church."

It was an open forum, and I was the new senior pastor. She had respectfully listened as I challenged the group to service while defining service narrowly as "ministry within the congregation." That is when she challenged me. I can't remember what I said. Most likely I mumbled something about not really meaning it—although at the time I did!—and then tried to move the discussion in a different direction.

In the days following the forum, I couldn't forget her words. The more I thought about them, prayed about them, and lived with them, the more true they seemed. Whenever and wherever Christians bring their faith to bear in service it is Christian mission—whether it is called that or not.

Many Christian disciples are called to serve in arenas outside the direct ministry of the church, be it in politics, education, business, social service, or elsewhere. The demands of their service may rob them of the time and energy needed to serve directly in church-based programs, but that doesn't minimize the importance of their service or mission. I had unintentionally devalued the role faith played in my challenger's choosing community service. She was right to call me on it.

Whatever the community of faith does to equip people for responsible discipleship and Christian leadership in the world is done in obedience to the God who loves the world and sends the church into it. The church is not a fortress against the world. It is a community of faith that exists in obedience to Jesus Christ for the world. Discipleship-driven congregations know this and live it.

Leaders Are People Too

I had asked him to serve on the ministry team that had responsibility for our celebration of the sacraments. Now he came to me with a heavy heart.

"Pastor Mike," he said, "I'm sorry, but I can't serve on this ministry team."

"But why?" I asked. "You have all the necessary leadership gifts, and you did tell me that you would love serving communion."

"It's true," he said, "but there is something you need to know about me." He hung his head and the next thing I knew there were tears running down his face. "Pastor, you can't have me up front serving communion because I am a convicted felon. I got into some trouble and embezzled from my employer."

"Did you go to prison and serve your term?" I asked.

"Yes," he nodded, "and eventually I made restitution to my boss. But you can't have an ex-con giving leadership to this team and serving communion. What if someone recognizes me?"

"Then they would know, Jake, that we practice what we preach. We are all forgiven sinners here. You paid your debt to society and your boss. God has forgiven you. Rather than being a problem for the church, I think your service will prove to be a blessing. You are, in fact, the perfect person to serve the sacrament that declares God's forgiving love to us."

I remember watching as Jake served his first communion. With incredible feeling he spoke the words of grace, "The blood of Christ shed for you." Jake, of all people, knew the truth of those words. Later he told me it was one of the most spiritually profound experiences he had ever had. Not just serving at Lord's Supper, but that, knowing about his past, I had still invited him to serve and to lead.

There are no perfect leaders. When we commit to growing leaders, we commit, like the Savior we follow, to taking them as they are and guiding them in the direction God would have them go. This is not an "anything goes" permissiveness. Rather, it honors the tension between personal responsibility, accountability, and God's forgiving grace. It invites real people, wounded and redeemed, into real service. Jake has since gone on to become a successful businessman and Christian presence in the community. His experiences leading in the ministry team and serving communion in the church were empowering steps toward building the necessary confidence for effective discipleship in his life outside the church.

Questions for Prayerful Reflection

1. Do you have a plan for identifying, recruiting, and mentoring new leaders in your congregation? If so, what is it? How is it working? If not, why not? How could you begin developing new leaders?

2. Does your congregation have an "authorization model" of lay ministry or a "control model" of lay ministry? What are the potential dangers of an "authorization model" and how can you guard against them?

3. Do you have ways of identifying and celebrating leadership outside the congregation?

4. When leaders experience failure, do you have ways of helping them "back into the saddle"?

5. Are "wounded leaders" acceptable in your congregation? If yes, what does that mean? If no, what does that mean?

FAILURE IS NOT FAILURE
IF YOU LEARN FROM IT.

9

Being what you say you are

"I joined this church for many reasons, Pastor."

The new member who told me this had worshiped with us and served on a number of ministry teams for at least three years before she and her husband decided to officially become members at Prince of Peace.

"I want you to know that among the most important reasons we decided to join is that we believe you and the other staff really live what you say you believe." She flushed—and so did I—and then went on to say, "I don't mean to suggest that you need to be perfect. It just matters to us that you all so obviously live your faith."

On the other hand . . .

"Pastor Mike," another member said, "I'm sorry, but we can no longer attend Prince of Peace. And we will be withdrawing our financial support."

It was a painful but necessary conversation with this woman and her husband, who not only loved the church but were also my friends.

"We just can't believe that you handled the situation with Mark as badly as you did," she went on. "There didn't appear to be any Christian love or concern in the way that you acted, and the aftermath has been nothing but pain for everyone. We wanted you to hear this from us directly." And they left.

Both of these conversations are repeated over and over in churches everywhere. In both situations, the bottom-line issue is trust. One family sees continuity between belief and practice, word and deed, faith and life on the part of the church's leaders and as a result invests their trust in them. The church is richer for it. Another family experiences discontinuity and even contradiction and consequently withdraws their investment of trust. The church is poorer for it.

Trust Is the Currency That Funds Ministry

Money is not the currency that funds the church. Trust is. No matter how big or small the church, when trust is broken, conflict and separation occur. When trust is present, the people grow, the church grows, and the work of God gets done.

Leadership thrives in a climate of trust. Yet it is easy to take that simple truth for granted. We assume that others will understand that what we do we do out of faith and conviction. We assume that others will automatically interpret everything we do as being done with the best interests of the congregation in mind. Those are large assumptions, and leaders ought not to make them.

Trust between leaders and followers requires:

- Authenticity
- Transparency
- Humility
- Vulnerability

A leader's personal commitments to discipleship and to the practices that undergird discipleship are the bedrock upon which trust is built. The word *authenticity,* for instance, brings us right back to the six marks of discipleship. Leaders who practice the marks in a disciplined way and seek to integrate in their day-to-day living the wisdom and strength that emerge from that practice are authentic. Disciples who "practice the presence of God" and let their love of God and God's love of them inform all that they do are authentic.

In community, authenticity requires *transparency.* Leaders cannot assume that people will understand what they do and why they do it. Their own commitments to discipleship and the practices that undergird it must be visible—not for show, but for trust. The relationship between leadership decisions and behavior and the beliefs, values, mission, and vision of the community must be clear—not to suppress debate, but for understanding and trust. Jesus provides an example. He both spoke and acted, and there was consistency and continuity between what he said and what he did. His words were interpreted by his actions and his actions gave meaning to his words. The result? Understanding and trust.

But we are not Jesus, which brings us to *humility.* None of us has all the answers. That goes with the territory. We are wounded, sinful, and finite creatures. Our woundedness and sinfulness often cause us to err in spite of our best intentions and our finitude means we have limits—limits to what we can know and limits to what we can do. Leaders practicing humility know this and turn their weaknesses and limitations into strengths by acknowledging them and seeking the advice and counsel of others. It is precisely at the point of our own weaknesses and limits that the gifts, strengths, and insights of others can shine forth. Humble leaders know this, accept it, and gratefully thank God for the ministry of others. Such humility engenders trust.

As I have mentioned repeatedly, both Christian leadership and Christian discipleship involve risk taking. This brings us to *vulnerability,* the fourth cornerstone of trust. An organization whose leaders will not take risks is like a ship dead in the water: still afloat but going nowhere. Taking risks gets us under way and moving toward our goals. Of course, it is good to remember that there are submerged rocks in the water—mistakes, errors in judgment, things we didn't know or overlooked—and from time to time we are going to hit them. You can bet on it. Leaders who are willing to be vulnerable, however, can stay afloat, make repairs, and get moving again. Vulnerability in this context is simple openness to admitting you were wrong, asking for forgiveness, and enlisting the aid of others in making things right. We tend to trust people who know when and how to say they were wrong.

> It is precisely at the point of our own weaknesses and limits that the gifts, strengths, and insights of others can shine forth.

Authenticity, transparency, humility, and vulnerability, the four cornerstones of trust, are the marks of leadership in a discipleship congregation. They are tied to the practice of the marks of discipleship and are clear signs of a mature spiritual life.

A discipleship congregation values trust because without it its capacity to accomplish its mission is seriously impaired. A discipleship-driven church, therefore, will set up institutional systems of accountability in which performance is evaluated in terms of the community's stated beliefs and values and is measured against the mission and vision of the church. All are held accountable for wise stewardship of the resources committed by the people of God for the work of God. Personal integrity in the use of money, time, and the material resources of the church is expected as a matter of discipleship.

In a wounded, sinful, and finite world, no matter how hard we try to avoid it, trust can be lost. Although the chances of losing it are minimized in a discipleship church whose leaders seek authenticity, transparency, humility, and vulnerability, it still can be lost. But the marvelous thing about trust is that it can be restored. This is particularly true in a grace-centered community of faith. In a community in which people have committed themselves to discipleship—and thus to having "the same mind . . . that was in Christ Jesus" (Philippians 2:5)—lost trust can be regained. Why? Because disciples want it to be so and struggle for it.

In times of conflict and wavering or lost trust, perhaps the best course of action for a leader is the advice given to me by a wise pastor years ago. "Outlast them, Mike," he told me. "Be who you are and just outlast them." In other words, in the midst of conflict and turmoil, continue the practices of discipleship, learn wisdom at the feet of Jesus, continue seeking genuine authenticity, transparency, humility, and vulnerability, and hang in there. Persevere, stay the course with integrity, and the gift of trust will be given again.

RESOURCES FOLLOW TRUST

"I am really uncomfortable with this," he said. "You are talking about blowing up our pledge system. How can we possibly develop our budget and financial performance plan without those pledges?" The president of our board was anxious because we were proposing a nonpledge stewardship drive.

"Well, I like it," spoke up another member of the board. "If we are serious about saying that we should give out of gratitude to God and in response to God's blessings, then what people will give is between them and God. I like it. It just seems to take our theology of discipleship seriously."

Remember, the currency that funds ministry is trust. The resources of ministry are an outgrowth of trust. When people develop trust in those who lead and serve them, their willingness to give of themselves in time, money, and prayer increases. When people believe that their leaders trust them, they respond with gifts of time, money, and prayer. When mutual trust waivers or fails, the resources for ministry dry up.

As I mentioned in chapter 5, at Prince of Peace we no longer use pledges. Instead, we teach about tithing as a mark of discipleship. The congregation trusts that the leadership of the church is committed to and practices tithing. The leadership trusts that the members either tithe or are moving toward a tithe as their faith and financial situation allow. The resources flow and ministry is funded.

Trusting Disciples to Give to God

"Pastor Mike, how much of my tithe should I give to the church?" she asked. "I mean, besides the church, there are other service organizations and programs that I support. Do I have to give them up?"

"By no means," I replied. "I thank God that you tithe, and as long as you are doing so, I would never presume to tell you where you ought to give. Organizations and projects that really care for people and so participate in God's love for the world are good places to give. I will tell you, however, that I believe a substantial part of your tithe ought to go to this congregation. Beyond that, I trust you and the Holy Spirit to work out the details."

I strongly believe that disciples should give to God through the church. The church, as the body of Christ, is the visible presence of Christ in the world. Without the generous and consistent giving of time, energy, and money by God's people, the church would soon become an invisible presence. Nevertheless, a discipleship church does not ask people to give to the church. Our giving is an act of discipleship, and therefore, we give to God. The church is critically important, but it is only one avenue for giving our time, money, and energy to God. When leaders let their people know that they trust them to give to God through the church, and that they support their giving to God through other avenues, most likely they will do both with glad and generous hearts.

It is a real tragedy when church leaders do not thank their people—and God—for all of their giving, whether it is given through the church or not. The vast majority of charitable giving is from God's people. Each year billions of dollars are given by followers of Christ to make the world a better place for all of God's children. But as long as our focus is only on what people are giving to the church we will not see or celebrate the tremendous impact our disciples are having beyond the church—nor will we thank God for it.

CONSIDERING RISK AGAIN, FROM THE PERSPECTIVE OF TRUST

"The wonder of this congregation," he said, "is that we continually come up against critical moments when we feel called to 'stretch' for the sake of mission far beyond what we thought we could do."

I had asked for a meeting with the past presidents of the church council at Prince of Peace. I wanted to know, from their perspectives, how this great community of faith had come to be. I wanted to be sure I was building on past and present strengths. So I asked, What were the significant gifts that God had called forth that empowered the church's growth? Who were the people who labored long and hard to build this community of faith, and what were their passions and dreams, convictions and commitments? I heard a lot that night. I heard about the innovative, evangelical ministry of my predecessor, Pastor Merv Thompson. I heard about the emergence of a strong laity committed to ministry, about thousands of volunteer hours in the service of God. They told me about creative programs and an ample supply of leaders to shepherd them. But here was something that struck me as somewhat unique.

"When faced with unusual or demanding opportunities, we have always been willing to pray long and hard and seriously consider whether God was calling us to risk or not. We haven't always had the certainty that we were called to step out on faith, to leap off the edge, and so then we haven't done it. But when we shared the conviction that God was calling us," and other heads around the table nodded in agreement, "we have always stepped out, trusting that God would meet our obedience with blessings far beyond what we could imagine."

When is taking a risk foolish? When is it faithful? I don't know. I'm not aware of any foolproof way to answer the question, although I do know that congregations that practice the marks of discipleship bring far more divine wisdom to the question than those who don't. In a membership-driven congregation, where the top priority is maintaining the organization for the sake of the membership, most, if not all, risks seem foolish. In a discipleship-driven congregation, where loving the world in Jesus' name is the top priority, what to others would be foolish risks look like simple faithfulness.

Discipleship congregations are prayerfully willing to risk. That willingness is rooted in the mutual trust that develops between people who have committed themselves to discipleship. When people know that the leadership of their congregation practices the six marks of discipleship and aspires to the four cornerstones of trust—authenticity, transparency, humility, and vulnerability—they are likely to support whatever risks are recommended as faithful to the mission of God.

Risk comes in all sizes and shapes, and sometimes what seem to be the smallest and simplest turn out to be the most complicated and dangerous. Or so I've been told by pastors who have tried to do something as "simple" as introducing a new worship option in a church that hasn't quite made the twin commitments to discipleship and mission.

> **Discipleship congregations are prayerfully willing to risk.**

Deciding to call another staff member when the money for salary isn't quite there, but trusting nonetheless that because the ministry is essential, the money will be there when needed, is a risk many growing congregations feel compelled to take. Still other vital congregations have risked moving to a different site to accommodate both growth and mission needs that are still largely on the drawing boards. Whatever the recommended risk, vibrant discipleship congregations pray about it, get the best information they can to make the best decision they can, and—if they are convinced that God is in it—they take the risk.

The discipleship model suggests that God can inspire any disciple to a significant vision that would entail risk. It becomes a "calculated risk" when

- it is shared with the community with passion but intelligence
- subjected to the common wisdom of the community and adapted where necessary
- affirmed by the leadership of the community as consistent with, if not demanded by, the beliefs, values, mission, and vision of the congregation

RISK REQUIRES OPENNESS
AS WELL AS TRUST

By openness I mean accessibility. If the system is appropriately porous, there will be multiple entry points for people to share their ideas, enter particular ministries, and help the congregation move toward the common vision. Membership-model churches are seldom porous. That is to say, they have few entry points—and those entry points are usually bottlenecks, not open doors, watched carefully by the guardians of power and privilege.

When people and leaders share the mission and vision, when they are grounded in the same basic beliefs and values, there is a high level of trust within the community. Such trust is essential for congregations to allow multiple entry points into ministry and mission. There is no power or privilege to be protected, just work to get done for the kingdom of God, and the more people doing it in creative and innovative ways the merrier. Once people begin to experience the porous nature of a discipleship congregation, they are willing to invest more of their ideas, time, and financial resources. Few people are willing to simply invest time, energy, and finances where their ideas aren't welcome. Trust them with the opportunity to help shape the ministry and mission of the community, however, and you are in for a power surge.

RISK FOR THE VISION

But when should a community of faith take risks? In a word, risk for the vision. If the vision is sufficiently captivating and grounded in God's intention for the world, it will create the need for such risks. Because vision seeks to partner with God in fashioning the future, vision always produces risk-filled moments. Rather than seeing risk-filled moments as potentials for conflict, they ought to be celebrated as evidence that the vision is alive and well. The power of vision is that it creates choice. Over and over again we will be confronted with choices when we keep the vision clearly in focus. The real danger is not in the risks we may take, it is in choosing to settle for something less than the vision for the sake of safety.

Even before we began to talk with our local YMCA about a program of exercise for body and soul, we knew that we did not have all of the resources necessary to underwrite the venture. Nevertheless, a burgeoning population of unchurched young adults and families in the area combined with an explosion of membership at this family oriented YMCA told us that we needed to reach out in a very nontraditional way if we were to move toward our vision of ten thousand passionate Christians in every generation. What began as the possibility of a short worship event followed by exercise opportunities has now grown into a full-scale worship, family fun, and exercise opportunity.

RISK FOR YOUR MISSION

At Prince of Peace, we have had a great preschool program called the Child Development and Learning Center (CDLC). Based on solid educational theory and adapted to the abilities of preschool children, the program flourished. Over time, however, the CDLC staff, students, and parents of students had grown to understand the program as largely separate from Prince of Peace. It began to occur to the leadership at Prince of Peace that if CDLC was a ministry of the congregation, it had to be more closely aligned to the mission of community. To redirect a "successful" program would be a risk, but we took it.

Over a period of three years, we began to change the program in ways that correlated with our mission statement. When we required that a witness to Jesus Christ be clear and evident through songs and Bible stories, conflict between the

CDLC staff and the church's leadership erupted. What began with the simple expectation that all of the ministries and programs at Prince of Peace key off of our mission statement turned into an unfortunate power struggle.

Later we learned that with more careful communication, openness, and trust between congregational leadership and CDLC staff much of the conflict could have been avoided. We learned from that failure, but taking the risk to be true to our mission was not itself a failure. Discipleship is for mission. In a discipleship congregation, everything you do must be mission-driven. Whatever risks you need to take to make it so are more than worth it.

RISK FOR YOUR BELIEFS AND VALUES

Some things are worth going out of business for—even in the church. If we cannot stand in faith, regardless of the risk, for the sake of what we believe, then our identity is in question.

As a congregation that has defined its ministry as "centrist," Prince of Peace must face the risks involved. Those on the theological left question whether we are truly committed to issues of justice and compassion. Those on the theological right question whether we are biblically faithful or not. Holding to the course we have set ourselves risks disenchanting either extreme, but to do less would be to surrender our sense of what God has called us to be.

In terms of its beliefs and values, a discipleship congregation must know what the bottom line is. Which beliefs and values are nonnegotiable, and what are those things about which committed Christians can differ in opinion? At Prince of Peace, that God created is nonnegotiable. How God did it is a matter about which Christians may disagree. That Jesus is God's only Son and the savior of humankind is nonnegotiable. Whether that requires a "decision for

Christ" is open for discussion. That the Holy Spirit is the active presence of God in our lives is nonnegotiable. How the Holy Spirit acts is subject to question.

Our beliefs and values have not been arrived at carelessly. We have searched the Scriptures for "golden threads," themes that run throughout and tell us who God is and who we are. We have discovered there a creating, redeeming, and sanctifying God, and we have discovered that everyone is included in the circle of this God's love. We have discovered that the church is called to risk all to tell people just that. We have found that disciples are people who follow the redeeming God by loving as God loves. And, with Martin Luther, we have no choice with respect to our values and beliefs except to say, "Here I stand."

A discipleship congregation will "wrestle with God" until it has a clear sense of mission and vision. It will fence with the two-edged sword of God's word until it has a clear sense of the beliefs and values that sustain God's people in the life of faith. And it will risk everything to be true to itself—even the risk that it might be wrong!

Discipleship congregations, knowing all about human woundedness, human sinfulness, and human finitude, avoid the arrogance of thinking they have final answers. They keep wrestling with God, searching Scripture, and praying. They hold the course but are always open to deeper wisdom, new understandings, and clearer vision—and that is risky.

STRUCTURING FOR RISK

Can you strategize for success in risk taking? I think you can. A strategic coalition to support healthy risk taking will be made up of three elements:

• the community's leadership, individuals who understand the relationship of the risk to the beliefs, values, mission, and vision of the church and vouch for its necessity

- disciples and friends who share the vision in trust and are willing to commit time, energy, and resources to overcome the risk and achieve the goal
- a team leader who will take charge, recruit the right people, and get things done

Without any one of these three elements, the risky venture will collapse like a stool with only two legs. With all of them in place, taking risks for the sake of the kingdom is an adventure in discipleship.

QUESTIONS FOR PRAYERFUL REFLECTION

1. Think about the four cornerstones for building trust in relationships. Are they areas of strength or growth for you?

	Strength	Growth
Authenticity	_____	_____
Transparency	_____	_____
Humility	_____	_____
Vulnerability	_____	_____

2. What might you do to turn areas of growth into areas of strength?

3. If trust is the currency that funds ministry and mission, how well funded is your congregation?

4. If resources follow trust, what might you do to increase the flow of resources?

5. Would you characterize your congregation as risk-taking or risk-avoiding? Why? What are the consequences of your attitudes toward risk taking?

MONEY IS NOT THE CURRENCY THAT FUNDS THE CHURCH. TRUST IS.

closing words

"**D**ear Pastor Foss," the letter began. "I'd like to briefly introduce myself to you. My name is Stacey. I'm 27 years old and a financial controller at AT&T. I enjoy ballroom dancing, my friends and family, and I adore children.

"I've been regularly attending Prince of Peace since I moved back home from Iowa three years ago. Since coming to Prince of Peace, I've been practicing the marks of discipleship. I pray and read the Bible every day. I also tithe my income—which, I admit, I struggle with every month. For me, though, it is a monthly reminder that Jesus is in the center of my life. My life makes sense to me because I follow Jesus.

"But, to the point of my letter. My mother had some very bad experiences in church growing up, and so she did not have either my brother or me baptized. If we were ever baptized, she wanted it to be our choice.

"I have believed in Jesus Christ as my savior since my early twenties. Now I feel like it is time to publicly confess my faith and enter the church through baptism. Your sermons have always touched my heart, and I am hoping you will baptize me.

"I realize you must get a large amount of correspondence. So, I'll give you a call in about two weeks to see if we can get together some time this summer.

"Thank you for your time. Best wishes, Stacey."

Make no doubt about it. We live in a spiritually confused and hungry age. People are looking to make sense out of their lives, looking for meaning, looking for connection to something greater than themselves. There seems to be a growing sense in our North American culture that the answers to our age's confusion and longing are somehow spiritual, somehow to be found in a transcendent reality that gives meaning and brings joy to the mundane and material lives we live.

Into this context, the community of faith issues the call to discipleship and authentic spirituality. Calling people to daily choose the ways of God and teaching them practices that attune them to the ways of God is at the heart of the church's mission.

The young person who wrote the letter above did celebrate and confess her faith in baptism. Her enthusiasm for that faith was infectious. When we first met, she smiled broadly and talked freely about what it meant to be a follower of Jesus Christ in a family that was confused, noninvolved, or nonbelieving. The water was poured, the name of God announced, and her faith was sealed by the Holy Spirit.

When I think of the church for the twenty-first century, I think of Stacey and others like her. They are all the reason the church needs for risk taking and creative innovation in ministry and mission. All of the men, women, and children who have no Christian history and no Christian memories are reason enough for making the move beyond membership to discipleship. Everyone who has ever fled the church because of bad, painful experiences or because he or she has found church boring and irrelevant gives us adequate cause to recenter our communities around Jesus and recommit ourselves to loving the world God loves.

Recently I was asked how I felt about the future of the Protestant church in the United States. I replied, "For the first time in a number of years, I am optimistic. I believe that the engagement of our people in ministry will continue to increase. Leaders will continue to surface. We will continue to witness to God's love made visible in Jesus with greater integrity and passion. The distractions of the 1990s are giving way to a nondenominational tidal wave of authentic faith, faith active in love, faith on the firing line—and the Protestant church will be revived because of it."

I still hold that optimistic picture months later. As we raise the level of expectations for followers of Christ, the Staceys of our world will engage, test, and declare for the gospel. I do not believe, however, that the transformation we seek is possible without a serious commitment to discipleship-driven congregations. The membership model of the church and its chaplaincy model of ministry are neither compelling nor powerful enough for the needed transformation.

THE WORLD IS NOT MUCH INTERESTED IN OUR DOCTRINES

"Surely you are not saying that doctrine no longer matters," the seminary professor said pointedly, as he responded to a statement made in a focus group designed to explore the future of the church and the role of the seminaries. His point was well taken. Of course doctrine matters. But it is a second-order concern, not the first order of importance.

There was a time when churchgoers demanded doctrinal clarity up front. Decisions as to whether to join a particular congregation were made in large part on the basis of the church's doctrinal positions. Denominations were clearly divided by differing theological emphases, and people—to the degree they understood them—paid attention to those differences.

With the advent of the postmodern world, this has changed. Among those who cross—or think about crossing—the threshold of the church, faith as theological propositions about God makes little sense and has no compelling power. People come seeking not theological argument but the experience of God.

Of first importance is a grace-full encounter with God through Jesus Christ. As a person's experience of God begins to permeate all of life, faith becomes a way of being in the world—a way of life—not merely a way of thinking or believing. When that happens, people are open to consider theology as reflection upon the experience of faith. Theology, after all, is lived faith seeking to understand itself. Faith as a way of life with God clearly involves a way of thinking about God and life. That's theology. It follows and then informs the experience of God. In the world in which we live, thinking about God cannot be separated from the experience of God.

> In the world in which we live, thinking about God cannot be separated from the experience of God.

Some of the theological shibboleths of the past, such as positions on infant versus adult baptism, are simply secondary in the minds of today's seekers. What is primary is the sense that in this place, at this time, I am in the presence of the Almighty One, the God who alone is God. So, folks who have called themselves Lutherans worship with Baptists and those known as Baptists find their way into Methodist or Presbyterian communities of faith. It is not so much an abdication of doctrine as an embrace of experience. As a result, fresh winds blow in dusty old denominational halls.

For congregations making the move beyond membership to discipleship, this phenomenon is a delightful challenge, not a threat. Effective communities of faith in the opening decades of the third Christian millennium will be those who commit to this discipleship model of the church, pay whatever price is necessary to achieve it, and boldly claim a place in God's creative, redemptive, sanctifying work in the world.

You Are the Light of the World

Let me conclude with a final story. I first met Jeffrey when he was just nineteen months old. He was battling childhood leukemia. When I met him, he had the distended stomach and patchy hair of a child undergoing chemotherapy. But Jeffrey also had smiling eyes and a shy smile that was nothing short of captivating.

For a number of months it was my privilege—and the privilege of my community of faith—to support Jeffrey and his mother through the arduous treatment regimen that eventually exorcised the demon of leukemia from his little body. Then he and his mother moved out of town, and I lost touch with them.

About two years later, I received a phone call from Jeffrey's mother. The demon was back. Jeffrey was in the hospital, and it didn't look good. She asked if I would come pray with him.

I made my way to the pediatric floor, checked in with the nurses, and then stepped into the doorway of Jeffrey's room. Looking up, he saw my suit and began to cry. Every other man who came dressed like that had pushed and prodded and made him hurt, and he had no reason to believe otherwise about me. Not wanting to disturb him more, I just stood in the doorway and began to sing "Jesus Loves Me" to him. He quieted and looked at me with those big beautiful eyes of his, and still from the doorway, I prayed for Jeffrey.

Two days later, Jeffrey lapsed into a coma. After several hours of sitting at her unresponsive son's bedside, his mother remembered having been told that hearing is the last sense we lose at death. So she went to the hospital library and found a children's book with a story she wanted her son to hear. Between tears, she read aloud to her son.

The story was about a little boy, like Jeffrey, who was in the hospital. The boy awoke in the night and, fearful of the darkness and strange place he was in, began to cry. The next morning another child who shared his hospital room asked him if he had cried the night before because he was afraid. The little boy said yes.

"The next time you awake and are frightened," his new-found friend told him, "just raise your hand into the air and an angel will come and take your hand and you won't be alone and afraid anymore."

That night, the little boy, once again afraid and alone, lifted his hand and an angel came and took his hand, and he died.

When Jeffrey's mom read that, all of the pain, all of the suffering—her son's and her own—flooded over her. Fleeing her son's bedside, she went into the bathroom and wept. After she had shed all the tears she could, she returned to her son and, once again, held his hand and wiped his feverish brow.

Hours later, with nurses, a physician, and the hospice worker beside her, she knew that her son would soon leave this world. Then, unexpectedly, little Jeffrey suddenly opened his eyes, looked over his right shoulder, smiled, and raised his right hand in the air. Then he died, his hand in the hand of the one who welcomed children into his arms and blessed them.

Finally, that's what this is all about. As Paul said in Romans 14:8, "If we live, we live to the Lord, and if we die, we die to the Lord; so then, whether we live or whether we die, we are the Lord's." The church knows that and is called to send disciples out into the world that the world might know it. Jeffrey's mother knew it, but there are millions who don't. Again, from Paul:

> But how are they to call on one in whom they have not believed? And how are they to believe in one of whom they have never heard? And how are they to hear without someone to proclaim him? And how are they to proclaim him unless they are sent? As it is written, "How beautiful are the feet of those who bring good news!" (Romans 10:14-15)

We normally tie this text to ordination and the pastoral vocation. That's a mistake. All who bear the name *Christian* are called to proclaim the gospel of God's love in Christ—and to live it. The one who said, "I am the light of the world" also said to his disciples, "You are the light of the world." As long as the world is a dark and hurtful place, God will continue to send disciples to bring light and love to those who dwell in it.

I commend to you the discipleship model of the church, the six marks of discipleship, and—above all—the life of discipleship. You will find in them a power surge for the community of faith.

NOTES

1. Plenary address presented in Lansing, Michigan, 1999. Emphasis added.
2. "Data and Trends," *The Barna Report,* October 19, 1998.
3. For a compelling treatment of the discipleship of the early desert fathers and mothers, see Roberta C. Bondi's two excellent books, *To Love as God Loves* (Minneapolis: Fortress Press, 1987) and *To Pray and to Love* (Minneapolis: Fortress Press, 1991).
4. John Kotter, *What Leaders Really Do* (Cambridge: Harvard Business School Press, 1999), pp. 51ff.
5. I owe this definition of spirituality and the spiritual life to my friend and editor at Augsburg Fortress Publishers, Henry French.
6. George Barna, *Turning Vision into Action* (Ventura, Calif.: Regal Books, 1996).
7. The Percept Group, Inc., can be contacted at 151 Kalmus Drive, Suite A–104, Costa Mesa, CA 92626.
8. John Kotter, *Leading Change* (Cambridge, Mass.: Harvard Business School Press, 1996), p. 85.
9. Ibid., p. 21.
10. "Centering prayer" is a modern term for an ancient tradition in Christian prayer. It is also known as "the prayer of silence" or "the prayer of the heart." Centering prayer uses the repetition of a sacred word, such as *love, peace, Abba,* or perhaps the name *Jesus,* as a means to focus the mind on God and still the heart from the distractions, worries, dreams, and mental noise that drag our attention away from God and hold it captive to less worthy things. It is an experience of the admonition to "be still, and know that I am God!" (Psalm 46:10). An excellent introduction to the practice of centering prayer is *Centering Prayer: Renewing an Ancient Christian Prayer Form,* by M. Basil Pennington (New York: Doubleday, 1980).
11. Jane A. G. Kise, David Stark, and Sandra Krebs Hirsh, *Life Keys* (Minneapolis: Bethany House Publishers, 1996).
12. John Maxwell, *Developing the Leaders around You* (Nashville: Thomas Nelson, 1995), p. 17.
13. Noel M. Tichy, *The Leadership Engine* (Nashville: Thomas Nelson, 1995), pp. xiv, 3. Emphasis added.
14. From a public address on leadership given in Chicago in 1991.
15. Martin Luther, *Christian Liberty* (Minneapolis: Fortress Press, 1957), pp. 30–31.
16. Martin Luther, "Preface to St. Paul's Epistle to the Romans," in *Luther's Works,* vol. 35 (Philadelphia: Fortress Press, 1960), pp. 370–71.
17. George Barna, *Data and Trends* (Ventura, Calif.: Barna Research Group, 1998), p. 1.
18. James C. Collins and Jerry I. Porras, *Built to Last: Successful Habits of Visionary Companies* (New York: Harper Business, 1994).
19. A good tool to begin with is the "Church Addiction Test" developed by Tom Bandy and found in his book *Moving Off the Map* (Nashville: Abingdon, 1998) pp. 50–53. Taking the test together with key leaders in the congregation is a great way to engage the leadership in a conversation about mission.
20. In a conference address at Prince of Peace in the fall of 1998.
21. Burna, *Turning Vision into Action,* p. 17.
22. Peter Senge, *The Fifth Discipline* (New York: Doubleday, 1990).
23. Tichy, *The Leadership Engine,* p. xiv.